The Jaguar XKs

The Jaguar XKs

A collector's guide
by Paul Skilleter

MOTOR RACING PUBLICATIONS LTD
28 Devonshire Road, Chiswick, London W4 2HD, England.

ISBN 0 900549 49 1
First published 1981

Photosetting by Zee Creative Ltd., London SW16
Printed in Great Britain by The Garden City Press Ltd.,
Letchworth, Hertfordshire SG6 1JS

Contents

No book about XKs would be complete without George Moore's famous picture of NUB 120 on its first Alpine Rally, in 1950. The headlights are covered to prevent damage from flying stones. *(Motor)*

Introduction and acknowledgements

The XK Jaguar sports car continues to exert a very great appeal to enthusiasts in all countries, and the inevitable rise in price of both cars and parts has by no means led to a diminishing of interest in the type — indeed, more XKs are being rebuilt now than ever before. If you are new to the car, this book may go some way to explaining why the XK exerts this appeal and what it is really like to own and run. If you already possess an XK, then I hope by learning more about the car you will be able to enjoy your ownership even more.

When it comes to thanking those involved in the production of this book, it must be remembered that without Sir William Lyons, his chief engineer for many years William Heynes, CBE, and all the staff and workforce at Browns Lane (and other Jaguar factories) there would be no XK to write about at all. So hopefully this book is another small tribute to the achievements of this team. I would also like to thank the present and no less enthusiastic management and staff at Browns Lane for the help and facilities extended to me in the preparation of this book, including Alan Hodge of the Special Facilities Department, and Roger Clinkscales of the Photographic Department, without whose help much of the authentic material and pictures which appear would not have been available.

Every author of a book of this type owes a debt to the major motoring journals such as *Autocar*, *Motor*, *Road & Track* and *Autosport* for their authoritative contemporary reporting and photographic record — all the pictures in this book are from Jaguar's own archives except where otherwise credited.

A number of individual owners of XKs have helped me, and I would particularly like to thank Rupert Arkell, whose recollections of all three types of XK when they were new have provided a mass of information about the detail finish of XKs, which is so important if an authentic rebuild is to be attempted. Not only that, but Rupert made available his present three XKs for the jacket photograph, and points out that the XK 140 roadster has yet to be restored, hence the unoriginal steering wheel and mascot!

Meanwhile, I am looking forward to getting my own XK 120 roadster back on the road after a couple of years' lay-off — I drive many types of cars in the course of my work, but nothing gives me quite the excitement and sense of pride in a fine British achievement as the XK Jaguar sports car.

PAUL SKILLETER

April 1981

How it all started — one of the **Swallow** sidecars with which Lyons first made his name. A variety of styles were produced, but the polished aluminium octagonal designs are the best remembered. This example, dated around 1926, is attached to an SS 80 Brough Superior. *(J. Allen)*

Most sporting of the SS 1s was the four-seater tourer. This is the much-rallied example belonging to A. G. Douglas Clease of *The Autocar,* and it sports a non-standard side-mounted spare wheel (usually it was positioned on the car's tail). *(Autocar)*

CHAPTER 1

Ancestors and parentage

From SS 1 to Mark V

Sir William Lyons — or plain Williams Lyons as he was before 1956 — had long been a manufacturer of sporting cars. But his first models were certainly not sports cars as we define them today. The SS 1 of 1931, the first complete car for which his company was responsible, equated more closely to what we refer to half a century later as a GT coupe. It was first seen at that year's motor show at Olympia, in London, where it caused a sensation on Lyons' stand, which was in the coachbuilding, as distinct from the car manufacturing section, as he had yet to be recognized as a motor manufacturer in his own right.

The car's impact, on press and public alike, was rather like that which might be expected today if, say, a relatively unknown provincial builder of glass-fibre specials suddenly produced a car which looked every bit as exciting as the best examples of advanced Italian styling, and announced that it was going into production and would be sold for not much more than the price of a Ford Cortina. The price of the SS 1 was to be £310, and there were plenty of takers.

It had been nine years since the formation of the Swallow Sidecar Company, with Lyons and his older partner William Walmsley holding equal shares. They had set up their business in Bloomfield Road, Blackpool, and later moved into larger premises in Cocker Street. There, a change of company name to the Swallow Sidecar & Coachbuilding Company acknowledged the expansion of their business into the design and construction of special bodies on various car manufacturers' production chassis, the first example being the Austin Seven Swallow, announced in 1927 and featuring an attractive rounded nose and tail in aluminium and an interesting hinged hardtop.

As the coachbuilding business expanded (Lyons' highly developed sense of style had quickly established the Swallow name as a leader in the field), the need for even larger premises and a more generous supply of skilled labour led to a further move, in 1928, to the Foleshill district of Coventry, where the range of Swallow-bodied cars was expanded to include Standard, Swift, Fiat, Morris and Wolseley chassis.

But Lyons had set his sights even higher. His trade contacts had confirmed to him that a ready market existed for a car with ultra-modern, long, low styling, but such a car as he envisaged it would need a purpose-built chassis. Accordingly, he approached John Black, of the Standard Motor Company, to supply him with suitable chassis-frames for what was to become the SS 1.

Later publicity made much of the fact that these chassis were exclusive to Swallow, but in fact they were not particularly special, and it was the flat springs as much as anything which gave the car its low look. The running gear was pure Standard, including the strong, smooth-running 2,054-cc six-cylinder engine (a less well publicized 2,552-cc alternative was available to order), which turned out to be just about the best part of the new car.

The original SS 1, with its long bonnet and 'cycle' front wings, proved to be none too durable so far as its bodywork was concerned, and owners of the 500 built were inclined to complain about bits falling off. But before a poor reputation was gained, the SS 1 was substantially revised, and the 1933 model was so much better that it was almost another new car — elegant, flowing wings now graced a body with enhanced proportions, largely thanks to the longer wheelbase provided by a new chassis-frame.

This was underslung at the rear and was provided with an 'X' bracing at the centre to increase its rigidity. Engine capacities remained the same, but horsepower was increased from 45 to about 48 bhp for the 2,054-cc engine, and from 55 to 62 bhp (at 3,600 rpm) for the 2,552-cc unit, thanks to improved carburation and a high-compression aluminium cylinder-head.

Performance was now beginning to catch up with the looks, and road tests reported up to 82 mph from the larger 20-hp SS 1, together with very acceptable handling. Meanwhile, for those with more modest tastes (or wallets), there was the SS 2, which had been based on the Standard Nine and had also appeared at the 1931 motor show. It had to wait until the 1934 season before it was revised, at which time it, too, was given an increased wheelbase as well as a larger 1,343-cc engine of 32 bhp, with a 1,608-cc unit as an alternative, giving over 60 mph.

Having sorted-out the basic chassis, the company, now known as SS Cars, then set about providing variety on the bodywork side by offering an open four-seater tourer version of the revised SS 1, which formerly had appeared only in closed coupe guise with dummy hood irons on the fixed head. Wings, bonnet and radiator remained much as for the coupe, but the two doors were given low cutaways for resting elbows, and the scuttle was given the characteristic 'thirties curved upsweeps in front of driver and passenger to deflect the wind when the windscreen was lowered. Then, for 1934, another body style became available — a genuine four-seater, four-light saloon, using the widened chassis and larger engines which Lyons adopted for that year.

Capacity was now 2,143 cc for the 16-hp unit, and 2,663 cc for the 20-hp engine, thanks to an increase of stroke from 101.6 mm to 106 mm (a measurement that was to become particularly familiar in the years ahead). Breathing arrangements were revised, too, and open four-seaters, in particular, now had a very brisk performance that was only bettered by much more expensive machines — 85 mph was just about within reach, and 60 mph could be gained within 23 seconds by the 20-hp car.

The first true sports car entered the story in March 1935, when SS Cars announced the SS 90. This was a real two-seater, carrying a typical mid-'thirties sports body with a multi-louvred bonnet, a small cockpit for the driver and passenger, and a spare wheel perched on the back (although the very first example had a rounded tail with the spare wheel inset at an angle). It was powered by the larger 2,663-cc side-valve Standard engine, and the aluminium-panelled body was set on a cut-down version of the SS 1 frame. Under favourable conditions, 90 mph could be approached, and like previous models from Foleshill, it offered tremendous value for money — the SS 90 cost £395, against over £700 for an Aston Martin Type C, for example!

But the SS 90 had scarcely entered production — some 23 were built between March and November 1935 — before it became out-dated. Lyons, quite correctly, had realized that the single biggest improvement that could be made to his cars would be to offer extra horsepower, and to this end he retained the services of down-to-earth Westcountryman Harry Weslake, already becoming well-known for his air-flow experiments and ensuing cylinder-head modifications on successful racing motorcycles and such as the Le Mans Bentleys of 1925-6. Driver-journalist Tommy Wisdom used to claim credit for his introduction to SS, who were being wooed at this time by Michael McEvoy with a Zoller supercharger conversion. Weslake's solution was to produce an overhead-valve cylinder-head for mounting on the Standard block; to the delight of all concerned this gave nearly 100 bhp, verified by Dick Oates, formerly of OM and retained by Lyons to monitor Weslake's results.

It was during 1935, when these engine experiments were well on their way, that William Heynes joined the company from Humber. He had been chosen by Lyons as SS Cars' first chief engineer. His initial job was to mastermind the installation of the new overhead-valve engine in the proposed range of cars scheduled for launching at the end of 1935, and generally to sort out their mechanical specification. These new cars were to be called 'Jaguars', a name chosen by Lyons from a short list drawn up by Ernest Rankin, his advertising and PR man.

The SS Jaguars made their first public appearance at the October 1935 motor show; there were four models, a 1½-litre saloon, a 2½-litre saloon, a 2½-litre open tourer along SS 1 lines, and a two-seater sports car. The saloons were handsome indeed, clothed in entirely new bodies and establishing a family line that would continue until 1951. The sports car was known as the SS Jaguar 100, and as can be guessed was a development of the SS 90, but now, with an overhead-valve engine to propel it, the '100' was a much more serious proposition.

Like the saloons, the SS 100 used an adapted version of the SS 1

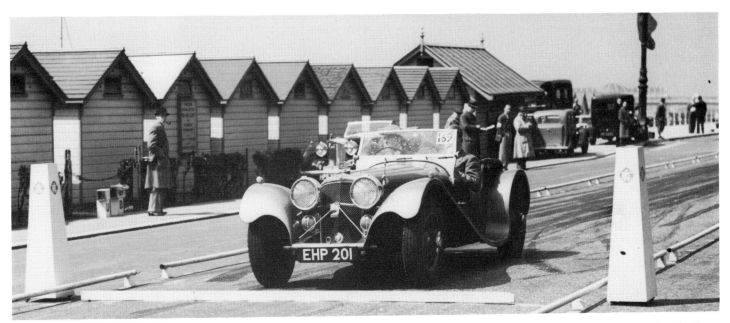

The SS Jaguar 100 — traditionally styled, but beautifully proportioned, extremely fast and very reliable. It was excellently suited to the type of road-rallies common in the 1930s, and this car is completing one of the seaside driving tests which were inevitably included.

chassis-frame — there had been no time for Heynes to design a better one, but at least he had managed to incorporate a number of improvements aimed at increasing rigidity and handling. Thus the side-members of the frame were boxed-in either side of the centre cross-member, and the region around the dumb-irons was stiffened. Unlike the new saloons, however, the rear springs were mounted outside the chassis-frame as extra width at this point was not important on the sports car. Both hydraulic and friction dampers were used at the front, with hydraulic only at the rear.

As installed, the 2,663-cc ohv engine gave a healthy and very reliable 104 bhp at 4,600 rpm, breathing through two 1¼-inch SU carburettors. The effect on its acceleration was dramatic — 60 mph was now obtained in 12.8 seconds, while the top speed went up to 96 mph. The '100' was a fast car by anybody's standards, and even the diehards were taking a second look at SS.

The next big hurdle came when it was found that demand for the new Jaguar saloons far outstripped the ability of the body shop to construct the bodies in sufficient numbers to supply the chassis line. This was because the coachbuilt method of construction had been utilized for the saloons, as there was no way SS could afford to have the body panels pressed in complete sections — the tooling cost for this was far too great. So each body had been hand-assembled from small sections tacked on to a wooden frame.

The bottleneck was overcome by redesigning the bodies to eliminate the wood frame and allowing outside contractors to supply the more complex panels. After a rather traumatic beginning, when some of these made-out parts failed to fit, the all-steel SS Jaguar saloon was put into production during 1938. With it came a further engine option — a 3½-litre power unit giving around 125 bhp.

While the SS 100 retained its SS 1-based chassis-frame (rather than adopting the much stiffer new frame designed for the 1938 saloons), it was provided with the 3½-litre engine as an alternative to the 2½-litre unit. Thus powered, the '100' was amongst the quickest off-the-shelf cars you could buy before the war. Furthermore, the cost was still only £445 (the 2½-litre '100' had been pegged at £395, or the same price as the side-valve SS 90). With the windscreen down, a genuine 100 mph was available, while the 0-60 mph acceleration time was a remarkable 10½ seconds. You virtually had to pay double for something which would out-accelerate a 3½-litre SS 100.

Nor was the chassis left behind by the extra speed. Though hardly an advanced design, even by the standards of the late-'thirties, well-chosen spring and damper rates combined to produce a very controllable car which could be power-steered round tight corners and held in a balanced condition through longer, faster bends. Owners and magazine road-testers soon

Tommy Wisdom in BWK 77, the works-prepared SS 100 which was increasingly modified by ex-Bentley man Walter Hassan and William Heynes; it eventually produced 160 bhp, which became the output aimed for when the time came to design a new engine for the postwar cars.

discovered that the qualities of the '100' grew more apparent as more miles were covered in it. The car even stopped well, thanks to the big drum brakes allowed by its 18-inch knock-off wire wheels.

Needless to say, the SS 100 made a fine competition vehicle, provided the events entered suited its 'road' specification — it was not built as a circuit car, but as an unstressed, reliable road machine capable of putting up very high average speeds without asking too much of the driver. In expert hands, it quickly proved its worth, even against top continental opposition, beginning back in 1936 with Tommy Wisdom causing incredulity when he won a Glacier Cup in the Alpine Trial that year with a 2½-litre model, having lost no marks at all on the road. This car, registered BWK 77, was to have a long and generally successful career as an official works rally and race car.

It was largely through an SS 100 that Walter Hassan moved to Coventry and into Lyons' employ. He had been developing Edgar Wadsworth's SS 100 while at Thomson & Taylor's, in the grounds of Brooklands, and this caused him to meet William Heynes, who assisted him with such items as high-compression pistons. An invitation from SS Cars followed for him to join the engineering staff (meaning Heynes!) at Foleshill, and he arrived there in 1938.

But by now, war was little more than a year away, and thoughts of the next generation of SS cars had to be shelved, at least for the time being, as the company was switched to the construction and repair of airframes and the production of trailers and sidecars for the armed forces. Nevertheless, some important work had been carried out by Heynes in the late-'thirties on independent front suspension systems, for it was clear that this was the way to go if William Lyons was to see his ambition to offer a luxurious 100-mph saloon, with comfort, luxury and safety, through to fruition.

Several ideas had been developed, and while SS Cars were immersed in war work, various independently suspended prototypes were kept in use and provided valuable information over high mileages, so that by the time car manufacture could be resumed again, in 1945, Heynes had decided on the system to be used for the new models which would ultimately replace the prewar saloons which had been brought back into production as a temporary measure.

This one-off design appeared on the SS 100 chassis for the 1938 Earls Court motor show and shows that the XK 120 fixed-head, when it arrived in 1951, had a true Jaguar styling ancestry. Indeed, many XK 120 styling features are embodied in Lyons' 1938 project.

At this stage, there was no serious intent to offer a replacement for the SS 100, nor indeed was the two-seater sports car re-introduced after the war, although ironically its greatest competition successes were to be scored in the late-'forties by Ian Appleyard, who took delivery of a 'left over' car which he used with great distinction once rallying was resumed.

In its final form, Heynes' new torsion-bar suspension was not dissimilar to the prewar Citroen's, though it differed in a number of important respects. Basically, it centred around a single lower arm, which projected at right-angles from under the chassis-frame to carry the stub-axle, the top of which was located by a forged wishbone with inboard mountings on top of the chassis-frame. The lower ('I' section) arm was triangulated by a strut, which ran forwards to mount under the front of the chassis-frame, effectively producing a wide-based bottom wishbone arrangement. A tubular damper acted on the lower arm, located by a pillar mounted on the chassis.

The torsion bar which sprang this suspension was splined into the lower arm and ran back alongside the chassis rail to an anchorage point in front of the chassis' centre 'X' bracing. This was one advantage of a long torsion bar mounted in this way — some of the input forces from the suspension were thus fed into the chassis at a point nearer the centre, instead of exerting even

more of a twisting effect on the forward part of the frame; it all helped to reduce flexing.

For connecting the top and bottom suspension arms to the hub, Heynes chose ball-joints — unusual at the time, but subsequently taken up by other manufacturers. Like giant rounded pin-heads, the ball-pins operated in sintered bronze cups, and because they allowed swivelling movements in any direction, they did the job of several separate joints and thus reduced the number of moving parts used in the suspension. The ball-joints (one top and one bottom) required regular greasing, but further routine maintenance of the suspension was cut down through the use of Metalastik rubber bushes for accommodating the up-and-down movement of the suspension where it mounted on the chassis — these also prevented the transference of noise and vibration to the car as there was no metal-to-metal contact between suspension and chassis.

As for the new saloon's rear suspension, this was more orthodox, but well thought-out. Leaf springs were used, but they were 6 inches longer and much more flexible than on previous Jaguar saloons, giving more wheel travel and a better ride. The live rear axle was damped by Girling lever-arm shock absorbers mounted on the chassis-frame. Heynes specified 16-inch wheels with 5-inch rims, their small diameter and wide rims being in the forefront of modern thinking at that time whereas 18-inch wheels had previously been considered usual for a car of that size and weight.

But advanced and efficient as the new suspension was, it was the engine — being designed at the same time — which was to be the star attraction of future Jaguars. There had been plenty of time during firewatching operations at the SS factory in the days of the 'blitz' for Lyons, Heynes, Hassan and 'new boy' Claude

Side elevation of Heynes' torsion-bar front suspension, as used on the Mk V Jaguar — the first car on which it featured; the hub has been removed to show the top and bottom ball-joints and the top wishbone.

An underside view of the new independent front suspension showing the torsion bar running alongside the chassis rail to the main lower suspension member, which is triangulated by the tubular arm in the foregound. Suspension members were rubber-mounted, as was the anti-roll bar also to be seen.

Baily to discuss how they were going to achieve the safe, reliable 160 bhp needed by the proposed 100-mph luxury saloon. Heynes favoured overhead camshafts from the start, though SS had not failed to be impressed by the 2-litre BMW 328s, which had proved such strong competitors to the SS 100, and a good look was taken at the BMW's engine to see how such a relatively high output was obtained from a modest cubic capacity — this was made easy thanks to Heynes' friendship with one of the quickest 328 drivers, Leslie Johnson, whose car was wheeled into the Foleshill works for close examination.

Gradually, various engine layouts were drawn up and then a series of experimental engines were built. Significantly, the very first of these (code-named 'XF') was a small 1,360-cc unit with twin overhead camshafts and hemispherical combustion chambers. It was followed by the 'XG', which used an opposed-pushrod method of operating overhead valves, leaving the camshaft in the block — this was to evaluate BMW practice, but its chief disadvantage was noise. Then came the 'XJ', more of a true prototype engine than a purely experimental one, having four cylinders, a capacity of 1,996 cc and twin overhead camshafts.

The 2-litre 'XJ' power unit served to prove all the major features which Heynes wanted to incorporate, with a variety of valve gear and camshaft drives being tried out, and the shapes of combustion chambers, ports and manifolds being experimented with — work in which Harry Weslake was vitally concerned. From it was developed a six-cylinder version, with bore and

The experimental engines which led up to the final XK engine included the XF (foreground) and the XG, which for convenience utilized the Standard 1,776-cc crankcase; the far engine is the four-cylinder XK power unit which was never to be used.

stroke dimensions of 83 × 98 mm and a capacity of 3.2 litres. This was to be the 'top line' engine for the new postwar Jaguars, but tests on the road soon showed that it lacked the low-speed punch of the older 3,458-cc Standard-based engine, even though it produced more power; the remedy was to increase the stroke from 98 mm to 106 mm, and thus was born the 83 × 106 mm 'XK' engine, which has been Jaguar's mainstay ever since.

Engine development had started back in 1943, just as soon as it was realized that the war would eventually be won by the Allies, so that by the time hostilities ended, in 1945, production versions of the XK engine had been built in both four-cylinder 2-litre and six-cylinder 3.4-litre forms. In fact the engine was ready well in advance of the car it was to power, as Jaguar Cars Ltd (as the company had been renamed in March 1945) were finding it a

struggle to convert their rather hotch-potch factories back to car production after years of war work, repairing bombers and building fuselage and wing sections. This meant big delays in getting the new saloon's bodyshell sorted out and into production.

In the end a compromise had to be made — the new chassis and suspension would be used for an interim model, which would carry a fairly traditional body not unlike that of the prewar Jaguars, which had been put back into production with a few changes after the war. This body would be made up of many small pressings, which could be assembled at Foleshill itself, just like all previous Jaguars, whereas the new saloon was to have a bought-out bodyshell manufactured in the modern way by Pressed Steel of Oxford, when eventually the difficulties and

The first 3,442-cc XK engine, photographed during 1948 in 'display' form with a polished sump and black-painted carburettors. Note the cast-alloy fan and the lack of a crankshaft damper, which were features of early XK engines.

The Mark V Jaguar, the 'stop-gap' car which used Heynes' new chassis and suspension, but not the XK twin-cam engine; this is an early drop-head coupe version with a three-position top.

expense of getting it into production had been overcome. As for a power unit, it was decided to use the existing 2½-litre and 3½-litre pushrod engines, the plant for producing which Lyons had managed to purchase from Standard; using the new XK engine in the interim model was not seriously considered because it would have been bad policy to use the new power plant in what was essentially an outdated body and, in any case, the XK engine production line was not fully operational by 1947-8.

The interim model was named the Mark V because, according to the press material handed out on its announcement, it was the last of five independent-front-suspension prototypes — but then Jaguar have never been very imaginative when it comes to model names! The Mark V was announced at the London motor show which opened at the Earls Court exhibition centre on October 27, 1948 when, despite its traditional looks and well-known power unit, it drew considerable praise and admiration. But not as much as the low, streamlined shape of the devastatingly beautiful two-seater sports car which was displayed alongside it!

CHAPTER 2

The XK 120

1949 to 1954

If there had been a little secret disappointment at Jaguar that the 1948 motor show didn't see the launch of the long-dreamed-of 100-mph twin-cam saloon, it must soon have been forgotten amidst the acclaim and excitement generated by the models which did grace their stand that year. The Mark V saloon alone would have made the Jaguar display a star attraction with its distinctive — if traditional — appearance, superb coachwork and sumptuous interior; the headlines, though, were generally reserved for a new Jaguar sports car called the XK 120 Super Sports. The '120', it was said, stood for the car's maximum speed — which in 1948 terms was a rate of progress normally associated with racing cars.

Unlike the saloon range, the XK 120 was not a subject of careful long-term planning; it was conceived, styled and built in only a few months, the display car only just being completed and made ready in time to accompany the Mark V on to the Jaguar stand before the opening day. As a publicity exercise it exceeded the factory's wildest expectations, and PRO and publicity man Bill Rankin must have been delighted at the exposure the XK 120 attracted within hours of the show opening.

The car owed its existence to the fact that the XK-engined saloon was delayed through the impossibility of getting its Pressed Steel-built body into production — the rolling chassis intended for the car was all ready and so was the twin-cam power unit, a very frustrating situation for Jaguar's engineering staff. Then came an idea — why not take this chassis, shorten it, place a two-seater body on top and turn it into a sports car? 'We agreed that as the engine was ready for production, it would be invaluable to have customer experience for 12 months before launching it in the new saloon', recounts Bill Heynes, who also

appreciated the publicity which would be generated.

The more it was thought about, the more appealing the idea became; 160 bhp with only a lightweight body to propel should produce a tremendous performance by the standards of the day. 'The Boss' was equally aware of the potential. 'Such a car with the XK engine could not fail to become outstanding', Sir William Lyons told me in 1975, 'as it should easily out-perform everything else on the market by a wide margin, irrespective of price'. The only problem was that Earls Court was only a few months away.

In engineering terms, the job was quite easy. All that had to be done was to take a complete Mark V chassis and remove 18 inches from the length of the frame side-members to give the suitably reduced wheelbase of 8 ft 6 in; the saloon's 'X' member bracing piece was discarded, the frame narrowed slightly and a single box-section cross-member inserted where the 'X' bracing had been. The suspension was not altered apart from some adjustment to compensate for the lighter weight of the sports car bodywork. No special testing of the assembly was necessary because all the road work on the preproduction XK engines had been done using Mark V cars with basically the same chassis — not that there was any time for such luxuries with the sports car before the 1948 motor show, and it is unlikely that the car on display (the very first XK 120 built) had any miles on it at all!

So most of the work centred around the body. Normally, this would have taken anything from eight months to well over a year to finalize and build, with Lyons — who styled *every* production Jaguar but one up to and including the XJ6 — having many prototype bodies constructed before deciding on the final shape.

The XK 120 rolling chassis, based on the Mark V frame with its massively deep side-members, but powered by the new twin-cam XK engine.

This one-off styling exercise arrived before the XK 120, probably having been completed by Lyons around 1946-7; move the headlights into nacelles either side of the grille and you very definitely have the makings of the XK 120.

The first completed XK 120 bodyshell mock-up has its picture taken round at the back of the Foleshill works. The car's beautiful simplicity of line is immediately evident.

No major changes took place to the XK's shape after the initial attempt; as these photographs were probably taken only a few weeks before the September 1948 motor show, there wasn't really time for second thoughts, anyway!

Yet the XK 120's marvellous lines were arrived at in just two weeks.

'It was done more quickly than anything before or since', recalls Sir William, 'and I could compare weeks, almost days, with years.' The shape was evolved using hand-formed panels placed on a 'jury' frame, these being altered and remade until Lyons decided the car was right. The official body development shop was busy sorting out the Mark VII body with Pressed Steel, so work on the sports car body was carried out at the back of the Foleshill factory near the sawmill, where Fred Gardner was in charge. Gardner was usually the man who worked closest with Lyons in these now-famous styling sessions, translating his ideas into metal.

When completed to Lyons' satisfaction, patterns were taken from the final mock-up for making the production bodyshells. Probably just one complete body was produced in 1948, this being the show car, which was handbuilt in aluminium — there was no time for tooling-up for larger-scale production and, in any case, no-one at Jaguar envisaged building more than about 200 cars in the first year. So it was with an aluminium-panelled

Door furniture and interior of the 1950 alloy-bodied XK 120; note the carpet heel-pad with cross-stitching and, just visible, the additional hump on the right of the gearbox tunnel for the starter motor, a feature of early cars.

The dash layout on a very early alloy-bodied car, with straight windscreen pillars. Steering wheels were almost always black on XKs, but white was an alternative seen occasionally right up to the XK 150.

A beautiful study of the aluminium-bodied XK 120; this 1950 car displays the curved windscreen pillars and large rubber grommets worn by the majority of alloy cars. Lights, bumpers, bonnet badge and hub-caps were all shared by the steel variety.

bodyshell that the XK 120 went into production when deliveries began in July 1949.

All the car's exterior panels — the aluminium front wings and scuttle assembly, rear wings and tail — were bought out, J. H. Cooke & Sons forming the panels on jigs at their Nottingham works and delivering them to Foleshill. There, in a very small work area away from the main production line, the body was pre-assembled on a dummy wooden chassis-frame before being lifted on to its own rolling chassis. The front wings and scuttle assembly were secured to the front of the chassis-frame by means of a transverse steel bar, which also did duty as a bumper iron — the neat little quarter-bumpers being bolted to it through the alloy wings — and further back by a steel bulkhead which served as the firewall. The assembly was linked to the rear half of the car by a composite wood-and-metal sill, which also supported the plywood floor of the cockpit. The rear half of the body, comprising the rear tonneau panel (boot surround), rear wings and spare-wheel compartment, was supported by a laminated ash frame.

Only the outer panels of the car were in aluminium — the front bulkhead already mentioned, the inner wings, which had to withstand stones flung up by the wheels, the internal walls of the luggage bay and the spare-wheel compartment (except the floor) were all in steel. The aluminium doors and boot-lid were wood-framed, but not the bonnet, which merely had a single bracing piece across its mid-point. This famous alligator bonnet was arrived at rather by chance — as the XK 120's shape evolved, it became obvious to allow it to hinge-up complete with the grille (which was a neat, chrome-plated affair with delicate slats).

At a time when American influence on British car designers was great, Lyons most laudably avoided disrupting the pure, clean lines of the XK 120 with an excess of chromium-plated fittings. At the front, that slim grille was complimented by two small quarter-bumpers mounted above air intakes for the front brakes, the 7-inch Lucas headlights with their 'Y' piece centres set into nacelles in the front wings, and the sidelights in their small streamlined plated housings. The detachable windscreen assembly was made up of two curved side pillars in alloy and straight centre pillar in brass, all plated. At the rear of the car were just two small lights, also in plated alloy, two vertical overrider-type bumpers, a numberplate housing painted body colour on the bootlid, illuminated by a Lucas reversing/

numberplate light, and a small curved 'T' handle for opening the boot. There were no door handles, the door catches being operated internally by a cord.

For a late-'forties sports car, the XK 120 was luxuriously trimmed and appointed. For a start the leather-upholstered seats were broad and soft, almost bench-type, in fact, and very unlike the small bucket affairs usually found in sports cars. Carpet covered the gearbox tunnel and floor, the doors had quite useful pockets covered by flaps, and there was quite a civilized hood, which disappeared neatly behind the seats when not in use, on top of twin boxes each containing a 6-volt battery on either side of the propeller-shaft cover. The detachable sidescreens could be stored in their own shelf, slung under the rear tonneau panel, when not clamped to the doors.

The driver faced a large-diameter Bluemel four-spoke steering wheel and a sloping centre dashboard with a useful array of instruments — large matching speedometer and rev counter,

The hood disappeared behind the seats when furled, on top of battery boxes. The seat frames on this late-model steel car appear to be painted rather than chromed.

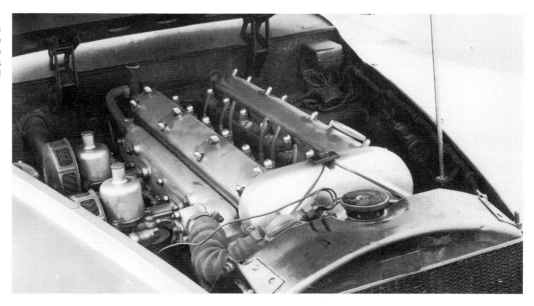

The engine bay of an alloy-bodied car, giving a good view of the early-type cam covers, which lack studs at the front. The makeshift plate bolted between the covers indicates the oil-seepage problems which later resulted in studs being added here, too.

ammeter, fuel gauge and combined water-temperature and oil-pressure gauge. The oil level in the sump could also be monitored as, by pressing a small plated button, the fuel gauge would indicate the quantity of lubricant instead of petrol. Ignition key and starter were, of course, separate functions (as they were to be on Jaguars up to the XJ6!) and a rotating switch controlled sidelights and headlights. The dipswitch was floor-mounted, and the pointed steering-wheel boss sounded the horn. A chromium-plated fly-off handbrake was positioned to the left of the transmission tunnel (or to the right in a left-hand-drive car), from which protruded a short, leather-gaitered gearlever.

Storage space was excellent for a sports car, and besides the map pockets in the doors already mentioned, tipping forward the seat squabs revealed a very useful luggage area (if not filled by the hood) and the boot itself, though shallow, was quite long. Underneath the removable boot floor was the spare wheel and a 14-gallon fuel tank, which was connected by a flexible pipe to a flip-up lid on the rear tonneau panel.

Under the long bonnet, of course, was that magnificent new engine, and an XK 120 owner needed little encouragement to open the lid and display the heart of the car — purposely, Lyons had requested that the power unit should look as good as it was, and it was equipped with polished aluminium camshaft covers, a bright aluminium inlet manifold and 1¾-inch SU carburettors, and deep, gloss-black vitreous enamelled branch-type exhaust manifolds.

As we have seen, the XK 120's chassis-frame was essentially a shortened version of the Mark V's or, more accurately, the XK-powered Mark VII's to come (there was no Mark VI because that designation had been used in the meantime by Bentley). In his technical summary of the Mark V on the occasion of that car's dealer launch, William Heynes described this chassis as, 'for its weight . . . probably the most rigid frame incorporated in any passenger car'; this was quite accurate and goes a long way towards explaining why the XK 120 was such a good car — designed for a heavy saloon, its chassis was exceptionally strong and rigid, which made for good handling and freedom from rattles and squeaks brought on by flexing coachwork. Compared with other sports cars from the same era, the XK feels very much 'all one piece' and gives a definite impression of solidity and strength.

The XK 120 shared similar braking equipment with the Mark V, namely Lockheed two-leading-shoe front drums and, leading-and-trailing-shoe rear drums — the 2LS front brakes were quite a new development and gave a self-servo effect, the shoes being pulled against the drum as it rotated. This, however, tended to aggravate what can only be called fundamental problems with the XK 120's brakes, which simply were not up to the speed of the car.

There were two major reasons for the deficiency in this department — the XK engine's ability to push the car to very high speeds between corners, and the small size of wheel used. The car's modern 16-inch wheels meant a relatively small brake drum (12 inches compared to 13 inches for the slower and lighter SS 100) and they also tended to shroud the brakes, making heat dispersal less efficient — especially as Mark V-type pressed-steel rather than wire wheels were used. At the rear, things were not helped by the spats which enclosed the rear wheels. It was not so much the very high ultimate speed of the XK 120 which contributed to brake fade, as the deceptive ease with which the car gained speed between bends, and it was the constant braking from around 70 mph to 40 mph every few seconds which really produced the dreaded brake fade.

The Mark V-type steering was a Burman recirculating-ball system, which gave a very compact turning circle of 31 feet for just on three turns lock-to-lock — a ratio which was considered a bit low-geared by some enthusiasts used to the rather more direct steering of prewar sports cars. But it made for light steering and found favour with lady drivers, and with both sexes in the United States, where four or five turns lock-to-lock were quite normal on home-produced machines.

In a way, the XK's steering highlights Jaguar's rather different approach to sports-car engineering after the war. The SS 100 had been strictly traditional — fast without frills and with few concessions to comfort. The XK 120, on the other hand, was perhaps the first truly *civilized* sports car, destroying once and for all the myth that if speed was required, sacrifices had to be made in terms of comfort and space. The XK 120 was not only one of the quickest sports cars of its time, but it had many saloon-car luxuries and was indisputably the best-riding — automatically benefitting from the pains that Jaguar had taken to produce a

suspension for their saloon cars which gave the best possible ride without affecting handling. People are inclined to remember the XK 120 for that 120 mph top speed, but the car's refinement was equally significant.

It certainly made an enormous impact on its first surprise appearance at Earls Court, and it received what was perhaps the greatest reception that any sports car has enjoyed at a British motor show — with the arguable exception of the E-type Jaguar! The car on the stand — the very first built and the only one in existence at that time — had the Chassis Number 660001, Engine Number W1001/7 and Body Number F1001 — all 'firsts', the '7' suffix to the Engine Number denoting the 7:1 compression ratio.

This show-stopper was finished in a subtle metallic bronze, with biscuit upholstery, and HKV 455 (as it was later registered) was really something of a preproduction prototype and displayed

First appearance. This is 660001 at Earls Court in September 1948; bumpers are low-set as brake cooling vents have yet to be adopted. Within days of the show opening, it became obvious that the original method of building the car would be far too slow.

This rear view of the first XK shows its unique lights and lack of both numberplate plinth and spat lock escutcheons.

HKV 455's boot, showing the interior petrol filler, unique method of securing the spare wheel (by a floor-mounted bracket, hence the hole) and plated boot hinges. Production-type bumpers and lights have now been fitted, however, for *The Motor's* 1949 road test. *(Motor)*

a number of features which differed from those on the production alloy-bodied cars which followed during the next year. Brake-cooling slots in the front wings were absent, the car's front bumpers being mounted down at that level instead. The rear-wheel spats did not have the external hole for inserting the 'T' handle for their release, and there was no fuel-filler lid on the rear tonneau panel, petrol being added by lifting the bootlid and using a filler cap in the luggage compartment, which led direct to the tank. There were no rear bumpers at all on the show car, just a thin, plated strip running underneath the bootlid, which lacked the numberplate plinth of later cars. Smaller rearlights were unique to the Earls Court XK, too.

Also catalogued at the time of the XK 120's announcement was a sports car which never saw the light of day at all. This was the XK 100, and it was simply the full-sized XK 120 powered by the 2-litre, four-cylinder version of the XK engine. The decision to market the sports car with this engine was even more last-minute than the XK 120 project itself, being taken just a few days before the opening of the show on October 27, the reason being that Lyons wanted to take advantage of — and associate the new sports car with — the high-speed runs that had been carried out by Major Goldie Gardner a few weeks before. Using the famous old

MG record-breaking car fitted with a mildly tuned version of the 2-litre ohc engine, he had achieved an impressive two-way average of 176.694 mph to give Jaguar's new intended family of engines its first piece of publicity.

As fitted to the streamlined EX 135 MG special, the 1,995-cc power unit — which shared the main design features of the six-cylinder version — gave 146 bhp at 6,000 rpm, while in normal XK 100 trim, the power output was quoted as 95 bhp at 5,000 rpm. With the 4.09:1 rear-axle ratio specified, this might well have been enough to give the car the 100-mph top speed which was hinted at, but it was never put to the test — demand for the XK 120 was so overwhelming that it was obvious within days of the motor show being opened that it would already be completely beyond the capability of the factory to make enough of the larger-engined car, let alone a second version.

So, although it continued to be catalogued for a season, no XK 100 was ever sold, and the nearest the car ever got to reality was probably when, much later in the 'fifties, a 2-litre engine was used in 'Lofty' England's own XK 120 fixed-head coupe for a while. In this instance there were no thoughts of production, but

28

Another early car showing how the tonneau cover was fitted; note also the short stalk mirror, which was another early feature.

the engine itself nearly saw service in saloon Jaguars on a couple of occasions — in the mid-'forties the company had serious intentions of producing a small saloon powered by the 2-litre unit, and later it was a strong contender for use in Jaguar's first unitary-construction saloon, the car which became known as the Mark 1; this, however, ended up with a short-stroke, 2.4-litre version of six-cylinder XK engine instead.

Meanwhile, with orders pouring in for the XK 120, it was obvious that something would have to be done about the frustratingly slow method of constructing the bodies, which was causing a real bottleneck. So plans were laid in conjunction with the Pressed Steel Company for manufacturing the XK 120's body on a volume basis, using steel panels throughout, though it would be 20 months before the revised body could enter production.

Fortunately, the steel-bodied XK 120 retained the original car's fabulous shape, though if you compare the two side-by-side you might be able to detect several small differences — the alloy car's headlight nacelles, for example, are stubbier, the leading bottom edge of the front wings under the radiator grille has a parallel line and does not slope inwards towards the grille as it does on the steel-bodied car, and the rear wings on the earlier car are slightly fuller. At a glance, though, the two are identical — but underneath the skin it was a different story altogether.

The new steel body had meant a total redesign of the shell, so that not a single panel remained interchangeable between the alloy and steel cars, except possibly the bonnet, doors and bootlid, which alone remained in aluminium. A completely new front bulkhead/firewall was installed, with different bonnet-hinge mounting points for the bonnet, which had been beefed-up with an additional bracing piece near the grille because of a tendency to crack. The bulkhead also incorporated a steel door hinge pillar assembly of new design, which did a good job of boxing-in the hinges, making them difficult to lubricate properly and even more difficult to replace when the pins consequently wore out and

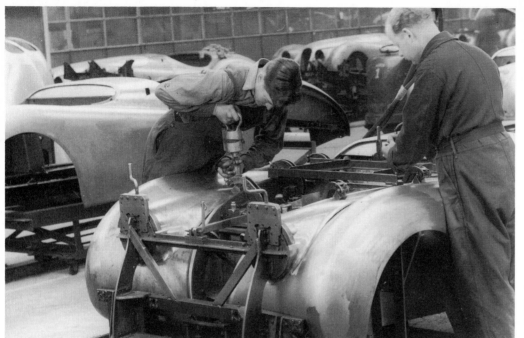

Building the steel-bodied XK. Here, the headlight nacelles are being fastened to the wings, and the wings to the scuttle, all the panels being held together on a jig. Afterwards, the joins were lead-loaded.

The Jabbeke event was celebrated by the production of these dashboard plaques signed by William Heynes; they were fitted to XK 120 roadsters for a while afterwards.

seized.

More complex steel box-section sills replaced the former simple wood/steel items, and the rear part of the body — with detachable, bolt-on rear wings as before — was now supported by a substructure entirely of steel. Interior and exterior trim remained the same, however, with the exception of the windscreen, which had slightly redesigned side pillars seated on thin rubber grommets where they met the scuttle — on the alloy cars (and this is about the only instant way to distinguish them from their steel sisters) these grommets were much thicker wedges of rubber. The first few XK 120s (18 right-hand-drive and 26 left-hand-drive models) had straight-sided pillars with three-point mountings securing the side pillars directly to the scuttle (rather like the SS 100 arrangement), instead of the pillars being extended below the skin to a more substantial single-bolt mounting point underneath.

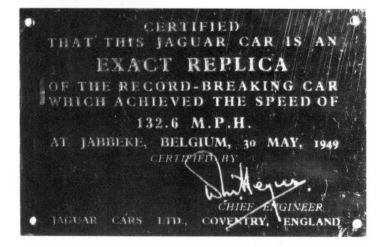

CERTIFIED
THAT THIS JAGUAR CAR IS AN
EXACT REPLICA
OF THE RECORD-BREAKING CAR
WHICH ACHIEVED THE SPEED OF
132.6 M.P.H.
AT JABBEKE, BELGIUM, 30 MAY, 1949
CERTIFIED BY
CHIEF ENGINEER
JAGUAR CARS LTD., COVENTRY, ENGLAND

A steel-bodied XK 120, this example being equipped with wing ventilators. This car has the longer-stalk rear-view mirror.

The rear view of the same car; note that the bumpers are fitted with the bulkier section uppermost — some owners get it wrong!

While the steel body was being designed and dies made, production of the original aluminium car slowly got underway. The first XK 120 to be sold left the factory on July 21, 1949 (Chassis Number 660002, Body Number F1005), was the second RHD car built and went to Jack Bryson's enterprizing Jaguar distributorship in Sydney, New South Wales. Australia was Britain's biggest export market at that time, and Jaguar in particular was to have great success there. America received the first LHD XK 120 to be sold, 670003, F1004 going to West Coast distributor Charles Hornburg, in Los Angeles, during September 1949. That was the month in which *The Motor* listed a home-market price for the XK 120 for the first time, though it had been announced at the show; the amount was an amazingly low £998, or £1,263 with Purchase Tax. By scraping in at just under £1,000 basic, Jaguar avoided a doubling of the still-new Purchase Tax, and the all-in price was unbeatable. The slower Aston Martin DB2 cost no less than £650 more than the XK 120, while the Cadillac-engined Allard J2, which could certainly beat the XK off the mark, if not match its top speed, retailed for a basic £1,200. People wondered — as they had for years — just how Lyons did it.

Deliveries, however, even for favoured overseas customers, did not amount to very many in 1949, around 60 cars being produced that year; most of the alloy-bodied XK 120s were completed during 1950, the last few just overlapping the steel-bodied replacement. The final alloy car in RHD form left Foleshill on May 1 for Singapore; its Chassis Number was 660058, its Body Number F1218. The last LHD example had been dispatched on April 12 (670184) and carried the last 'alloy' Body Number F1240 (Body Numbers did not run in sequence with Chassis Numbers). Exactly 240 alloy-bodied cars were built, or considerably fewer than the total SS 100 production before the war.

Two chassis had been taken from the 'alloy' series for prototype steel-bodied XK 120s, which explains the 242 Chassis Number total; the first steel-bodied car to be sold in RHD form was 660059 (Body Number F1264) and it went to Australia on April 20, 1950. The first steel-bodied car sold in LHD form (670185, F1244) went overseas on May 19. But demand for the car was still insatiable due both to its visual appeal and to the fact that the XK 120 was quickly proving to be as fast on the road as it looked attractive in the showroom.

That it was perfectly capable of living up to its type number was proved quite early on, thanks to a demonstration laid on by Jaguar in Belgium for the benefit of the press. This took place in May 1949 on the Jabbeke-Aeltre autoroute which, conveniently, was both long and straight and didn't lead anywhere, which meant that it was quite easy to persuade the authorities to close it for record-breaking — Goldie Gardner had used it for his runs with the Jaguar-powered EX 135 only nine months previously. But the vehicle used on this occasion was a true, standard XK 120, registered HKV 500 and the second LHD car built.

Its driver was Ron Sutton, who had been somewhat tentative about both his ability to conduct the XK 120 at its maximum and the true nature of its top speed, but a dress rehearsal in the early hours on quiet roads near Coventry proved satisfactory on both counts, so off went HKV 500 to Belgium. To watch went a party of 20 or so journalists in a Dakota chartered by Lyons, who didn't mind spending money if the occasion was right. He certainly got his money's worth on this occasion, for the sleek white XK 120 proceeded to fly down the autoroute at a two-way average of 126.448 mph with hood and sidescreens erected, and at no less than 132.596 mph with the hood and windscreen removed and the addition of an undertray!

It is difficult to appreciate today how stunning these figures were for a production, road-going sports car that could genuinely be purchased — albeit after a considerable wait — from any one of hundreds of retail outlets all over the world. The speed of 120 mph represented the maximum of a normally-geared ERA, then Britain's most successful single-seater racing car, and 130 mph about the very best that a production Bugatti could manage before the war.

Indeed, this very topic provoked a lengthy series of correspondence in *The Motor* as Jaguar and Bugatti adherents fought it out. It ended with a letter from Forrest Lycett, master of the 8-litre Bentley of another era, who had driven an XK 120 ('I have seen 5,000 rpm in top in a semi-suburban area') and who

Interior of the production steel-bodied XK; this fairly early car has the plated seat frames and a 'short-reach' hood, as indicated by the plated anchorages on the rear tonneau panel.

stated that in his opinion there was 'nothing in any degree comparable' with the XK 120 at the price. 'The gratitude of Britain at the present economic juncture is due to all engaged in the production of this remarkable car', he concluded. The achievements of these early XK 120s (including their successful racing debut at Silverstone later in 1949 — see Chapter 6) were indeed received with a national sense of pride, and the international publicity they gained did much to bolster the standing of the entire British motor industry at a time when such encouragement was much needed.

Subsequent independent road tests by British and other journals confirmed that the Jabbeke runs were fairly representative of off-the-shelf XK 120s. *The Motor* achieved 124.6 mph with HKV 455, the very first XK 120, Harold Hastings recalling of the occasion that due to the phenomenally high speeds that were involved, the Temple Press management insisted that it should be his unmarried colleague Joe Lowrey who must conduct the car on the high-speed runs! This did not

prevent Hastings from achieving his personal 120 mph with the car on a later occasion in the test — and he relates that the experience was, in a sense, disappointing because of the sheer stability of the car and its total lack of drama at such a speed.

The acceleration of the XK was highly impressive, too, being quite beyond the experience of most drivers in those days, 0-60 mph being covered in 10 seconds exactly; the car even managed a 0-100 mph time of 44.6 seconds using top gear only! As a bonus, an overall fuel consumption of 19.8 mpg was recorded, so that car was far from being a thirsty monster. *The Motor's* road test aroused a good deal of interest because the figures gained were the first to be recorded independently; previously, Bill Rankin had been reluctant to lend the journal a car, despite repeated requests, but he had had to give in, Harold Hastings relates, due to sheer pressure from the public, who wanted to know if the Jabbeke runs had been verified by an outside source.

The Autocar was eventually given the chance to test an XK 120

The superb C-type Jaguar, or XK 120C, which was built around a tubular chassis-frame in time for the 1951 Le Mans race — which it won impressively to give Jaguar their first of five victories in the French classic.

as well, in April 1950. The car tried was JWK 675, and was the first steel-bodied XK built (670172), which means that a direct comparison can be made between the performances of the steel-bodied and alloy-bodied cars. In fact JWK 675 — a left-hooker — was a little slower than the prototype XK 120, with a 0-60 mph time of some 12 seconds. This was undoubtedly due to its extra weight, although the increase, in the region of 1 cwt, was not too much considering that XKs are heavy cars anyway at around 25½ cwt for an alloy example and 26½ cwt for a steel-bodied two-seater. Unfortunately, *The Autocar* did not attempt a maximum-speed run, but others — including Bill Boddy of *Motor Sport* — reckoned that a stock production XK 120 roadster, with the 7:1 compression ratio, was good for 110 mph.

The few who were fortunate enough to get delivery of an XK 120 in those early-postwar years revelled in this sort of performance. Alex Moulton, famous for his rubber suspension designs (as used on the original Mini) bought one and had this to say of it in 1964: 'I remember doing a long trip in France in the thing and it was fun seeing 100 mph come up on the speedometer and stay there for long periods. In those early days it was quite an experience. But I couldn't manage it at all in the wet. It was quite before the comprehension of tyre requirements we have today.'

Not that the XK 120 was an uncontrollable beast — its handling, in fact, was very predictable and forgiving, with initial mild understeer, then an easily managed tail slide if the car was cornered really hard. A slightly more sudden breakaway might,

The C-type used a great many XK 120 components, as this 1951 picture shows, including the wishbone-and-torsion bar front suspension and a mildly tuned version of the 3.4-litre XK engine, still running on 1¾-inch carburettors that year.

The aeroscreens and mirror cowl, which could be bolted to the scuttle in place of the normal windscreen. Note the early XK 120's dangerous-looking horn push — as these early cars had no indicators, a Mark V assembly was used and turned upside-down so that the indicator switch slot was hidden.

Rear view of a Special Equipment roadster, showing the twin exhaust pipes and giving a good view of the XK 120's small rear window.

however, occur in the wet because the skinny, hard-rubber tyres of the day simply couldn't cope with the power on tap; but this was by no means dangerous. Of course, a properly designed suspension was the chief reason for the XK 120's good handling qualities, and later it proved perfectly able to cope with an additional 50 bhp with no alteration as development of the XK series continued. About the only criticism that initially could be directed at the car in this respect was the unsporting amount of roll, but even this was soon tackled by Jaguar, who issued a list of bolt-on performance and handling parts in mid-1951.

By this time the C-type Jaguar, based on production XK 120 parts in a tubular frame, had been built. From the experience gained with this car, and with the unofficial 'works' XK 120s which had clocked up numerous successes in the meantime, the factory was able to evolve a number of modifications and suggestions aimed at improving the XK 120 for racing, rallying or fast road use — and a high proportion of owners at that period, both in Britain and abroad, indulged in some form of competition activity with their XK 120s.

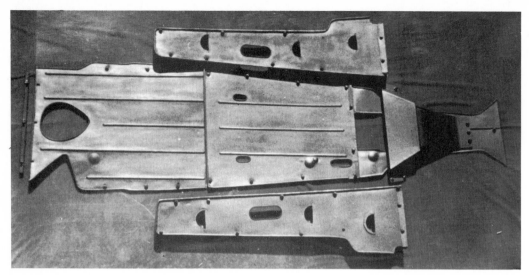

A very rare performance option was the undershield assembly. Possibly the only surviving example is kept by XK 120 owner Paul Borel in the United States. *(Paul Borel)*

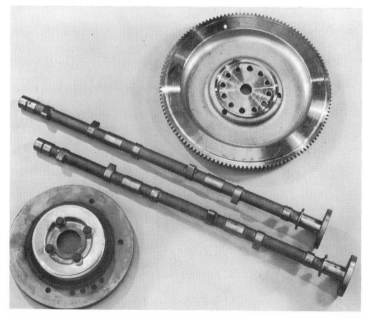

The lightened flywheel, high-lift cams and crankshaft damper, which featured in the Special Equipment engines.

For a start, a useful power increase could be gained from fitting sets of 8:1 or even 9:1-compression pistons, now that better-quality fuel was becoming available. The carburettors could be rejetted, and a high-lift camshaft was listed, giving a 3/8-inch lift as opposed to 5/16-inch (its appearance in the XK engine had only been delayed because of misgivings at the factory about the possibility of careless servicing, for when the high-lift cam was fitted, the valves could touch and become bent if the camshafts were turned out of sequence). A dual exhaust system incorporating a Burgess straight-through silencer could be obtained, a lighter flywheel gave a quicker response to the throttle, a crankshaft damper more suited to higher rpm could be specified, and a solid-centre clutch fitted to deal with the transference of power.

With all the 'special equipment' in place, an 8:1 engine now gave 181 bhp at 5,800 rpm, instead of 160 bhp at 5,400 rpm, and to accommodate the increased pace, optional stiffer torsion-bars (1/16-inch larger diameter) and thicker rear spring leaves could be installed to reduce roll. Nothing was done about the brakes, although owners were advised that air-scoops could be fitted to the rear brakes. Aeroscreens with neat aluminium cowls (plus one for the mirror) were available, as were lightweight bucket seats in Bedford cord or leather; a full-length undershield was also listed, but rarely supplied — I know of only one in existence (this should not be confused with the sump deflector assembly, Part Number C5106, which was available to order from April 1950 as a guard for the sump on cars used in rough conditions, especially overseas).

An XK 120 with full optional equipment was a delightful and extremely potent sports car, capable of reaching 60 mph in around 8½ seconds — indeed, a competitive club racer or potential national rally winner with little extra work. Only the brakes were overworked, and these were assisted when, during 1951, wire wheels became optional. An unofficial Borrani alloy-rim conversion had previously been marketed in the United States by Alec Ulmann, but the official works item retained the pressed-steel wheel's 16 × 5-inch dimensions and were of 54-spoke construction; cars so equipped were sold without rear-wheel spats because these would have fouled the large chromium-plated 'spinners'. In May 1952, the pressed-steel wheels were given an extra ½-inch rim width and strengthened, bringing them into line with the Mark VII saloon, but wire wheels on XKs always featured 5K rims.

Performance equipment apart, it is remarkable how little the XK 120 needed to be changed after the steel-bodied cars entered production. Thanks, perhaps, to the extra time allowed for testing by lack of car production during the war years, suspension and engine were 'right' from the very start and required only detail changes after the car went into service. The more important of these are listed in the Appendices — there was some experimentation with the material for the suspension ball-joints, and with timing-chain tensioners in the engine, but nothing fundamental needed alteration as both the XK engine and the car itself proved tough and reliable. As a 'test-bed' for the XK power unit, the XK 120 had almost been unnecessary!

Early in March 1951, the appeal of the XK 120 had been further widened through the introduction of a fixed-head coupe; its major styling features bore an even more uncanny resemblance to Lyons' one-off closed SS 100 of 1938 than had the roadster, but it was considerably more graceful and some think that it is the most beautiful XK of all. An identical wing line to that of the open car was retained; with a fixed head embodying Mark VII

styling features neatly blended into the scuttle and rear tonneau panel.

The interior of the fixed-head coupe also followed the Mark VII pattern, as although the seats looked similar to the roadster's, the doors had wind-up windows and wood cappings; the dashboard and facia were also in walnut veneer, giving the car a very opulent air. A glovebox was provided for the passenger, transparent tinted

The optional bucket seats for the XK 120; these examples are installed in the ex-Dick Protheroe car, CUT 6.

A lovely study of a late-model Special Equipment XK 120 open two-seater, with factory chrome wire wheels. Note that the sidelights are now integral with the front wings.

An early XK 120 fixed-head coupe with side exhaust; this car was a true 'business man's express'.

XK 120 front suspension carrying splined hubs for wire wheels. Brake drums on these cars were dished at the front but not at the back. Wire wheels improved the XK 120's braking performance considerably, thanks to the extra ventilation.

This is almost certainly the prototype XK 120 fixed-head, and it displays non-standard items like the semaphore indicator instead of a vent in the wing and an upright side-window pillar.

Front view of an export fixed-head showing how the original XK's lines were enhanced by the new body style. The car's Chassis Number (680088) is chalked on the screen — I wonder if this car survives?

The fixed-head's roofline was very similar to that of the Mark VII saloon — certainly pure Jaguar. The rear window was inconveniently small in the fashion of the day.

sun-visors were fitted and there were two recessed interior lights adjacent to the rear window. A further innovation, also introduced on the open car from the same date, was the fitting of footwell ventilators; these took the form of hinged flaps let into the sides of the front wings, and were mainly for the benefit of owners living in more equatorial realms — heat from the engine in front and from the transmission at the side could turn even the open car into a fair imitation of a low-bake oven!

On the subject of heat, in cold weather a certain amount could be supplied by an optional heater unit; it was not very efficient, but it was better than nothing. In November 1951 it was standardized for the roadster as well, but the open car lacked the additional demist facility, with vents let-in at the base of the windscreen, until almost a year later. The fixed-head coupe also introduced body colour sidelight pods which were integral with the front wings, and the separate chrome-housing type were discontinued on the open cars in October 1952. As a further convenience, cars were now being wired for flashing indicators, and where fitted, the system used double-filament bulbs in the sidelights and the indicators were operated by a manette control

Jaguar also borrowed from their saloons for interior furnishings for the XK fixed-head; besides the wood-veneer dash and cappings, this view also shows the translucent plastic sun visors.

in the steering wheel boss, similar to the arrangement provided for the Mark VII.

Upholstery differed from early XK 120 open-two-seaters by virtue of being trimmed in leather of one colour — previously, the outer panels of the seat covers had been in a darker colour (for example red surround, beige inner). A similar shade was used for the carpets, door trim and piping under the dashboard (the dash itself was in the lighter hue). The only exception appears to have been roadsters finished in silver, where the interior trim colour was all red, and it was this scheme which was adopted by Jaguar for the closed car (in a selection of colours, naturally).

Despite pleas from the United States, Jaguar stuck to a strict two-seater policy for the new model — there really was insufficient space for 'occasional' rear seats and the available space behind the front seat squabs was used for a shallow locker, which could be swung down for access to the twin 6-volt batteries underneath.

Mechanically there were few changes, though the optional

No rear seats yet, just a shallow locker, which was swung down to show the twin six-volt batteries. The 'funeral' rail on top was not standardized for production.

As with the roadster, the painted body was dropped on to the fully-equipped chassis by a sling, after which the assembly would pass down the line (by this time at Browns Lane, Allesley, where the factory moved during 1951) for wiring-up and trimming.

The drop-head XK 120, with its beautifully tailored folding head; this car was produced during a nickel shortage and sports painted rearlight bodies. It also has a non-standard semaphore indicator.

'speed' goodies were now assembled as a factory package to create a new model of fixed-head coupe and roadster — the Special Equipment version, which incorporated the high-lift cams, dual exhaust system, 8:1 compression ratio and wire wheels.. *The Autocar* discovered that in this trim, the 27-cwt closed XK managed 60 mph in 9.9 seconds and could achieve the magic 120-mph figure.

There was also a useful improvement in braking power, thanks to the adoption of self-adjusting front brakes in April 1952 after only a few fixed-head coupes had been sold (three in RHD and 622 in LHD form); the roadster also benefitted from this development, which had been proved on the 1951 C-type. It consisted of two adjuster bars linking the brake shoes, the bars being pulled over friction pads as the shoes were forced against the drum. With the aid of a ratchet device, when the brakes were released the bars allowed the shoes to return only to the correct

The drop-head with the top down and covered by its envelope; this is a Special Equipment example with painted wire wheels.

lining/drum clearance. This overcame the original system's tendency to produce a longer and increasingly ineffectual brake-pedal travel as the brake linings wore and the cast-iron drums heated-up and expanded during frequent hard use of the brakes.

A tandem master-cylinder was also now fitted, giving a measure of fail-safe braking should front or rear hydraulic circuits be rendered inoperative. The whole set-up, especially in conjunction with wire wheels, which allowed much better circulation of cool air, produced a worthwhile increase in the XK 120's braking reserves; but the problem of fade was far from solved — and it was known that Jaguar and Dunlop were working jointly on a new type of brake that dispensed with brake shoes and drums altogether.

In April 1953, the third and final XK body style came into being. This was the drop-head coupe, and it combined the sophistication and opulence of the closed car with the wind-in-

'Over-centre' toggle catches were used to secure the drop-head's top to the windscreen rail.

A good view of the XK 120 drop-head's rear window in its zipped panel. Note also the headlining and interior light.

the-hair appeal of the roadster, thanks to a beautifully tailored folding head. Much more than a simple hood, it was what is termed a 'wig top' in the trim shop, exactly emulating the contours of the fixed-head's metal roof thanks to layers of horse-hair padding under the mohair outer covering. It was fully lined inside, and even boasted an interior light, while the rear window could be unzipped for extra ventilation with the top up (the same facility had been adopted on the open car's more primitive hood in January 1953). The doors (still in aluminium) were given proper wind-up windows and opening quarter-lights set in chromium-plated brass frames.

The top worked beautifully — when it was erected there was little difference in refinement between the drop-head and fixed-head cars, while manipulating it was easy, with just three chromium-plated over-centre toggle catches securing the head to the top of the non-detachable windscreen frame. These could be released from the driving seat, after which the top would drop down neatly behind the seat squabs, the wood-capped cantrails parting and folding themselves neatly as they descended. Two plated hooks prevented the hood from catching the wind when down, and the assembly was covered by a nicely tailored and lined hood envelope when in its folded position.

Interior trim was very similar to that of the fixed-head coupe, though duo-tone upholstery colours were mainly used. Mechanically there were no changes, except that all drop-heads used the Salisbury rear axle in place of the ENV item. The former

An XK 120 roadster equipped with the big 2-inch SU H8 carburettors and C-type head — although the latter didn't carry the camshaft plate stating the type until the advent of the XK 140.

XK 120 roadster with full Special Equipment, plus big Lucas spotlamps in addition; the driver is a youthful Bob Berry, destined for a long and successful career within the motor industry, and the car also led an active life, which included rallying and high-speed runs at Jabbeke.

had been gradually phased-in on the earlier XK models since November 1952, at first in 2HA form with the slightly lower ratio of 3.77, then, when the 4HA type was standardized for all cars on the introduction of the drop-head in April 1953, with a 3.54 ratio, which gave virtually the same gearing as the original 3.64 of the ENV axle. Alternative ratios available to special order were 4.09, 3.77, 3.31, 3.27 and the very high 2.93:1. The Salisbury axle can be distinguished from the ENV type by its large hub nut, visible on removing a hub cap.

Also in April 1953 came the availability in limited quantities of a further important tuning part — the C-type cylinder-head. On outright sale only, it came complete with high-lift cams and

On the concours circuit — and it is at events like this that you mostly see XK 120s today; this is Ed and Karen Miller's 1952 roadster, with appropriate New York registration and looking particularly attractive with light-coloured top and Rim-bellishers on the wheels. *(Claus Rossin, Empire Division JCNA)*

valves, but without manifolds — the owner could either refit his existing manifolds, including the 1¾-inch SU carburettors, or opt for the purchase of a special manifold and two 2-inch carbs. Thus the new range of parts were:

Part Number		Retail price
SD 1025	Cylinder-head assembly	£150
C 6007	Manifold	£6 13s 0d
C 7095	Front carburettor, 2-inch	£18
C 7096	Rear carburettor, 2-inch	£18

The cylinder-head was based on that used for the C-type sports-racing car; the inlet valve size remained at 1¾-inch (in fact this diameter was never to vary on production Jaguars until the fuel-injected XJ6 engine of May 1978), but the exhaust valve diameter was increased from 1 7/16-inch to 1 5/8-inch. Both inlet and exhaust porting was enlarged, and in conjunction with 8:1 pistons and two 1¾-inch carburettors, the C-type head was rated at 210 bhp at 5,750 rpm. While you could order it on your new XK 120 straight from the factory, it was never incorporated in the specification of a catalogued model, as were the items which made up the normal Special Equipment XK 120s (the latter was known as the XK 120M in the United States, 'M' denoting 'Modified').

The sporting driver could also order 'alternative constant-mesh gears' by the spring of 1953, which provided closer intermediate gear ratios; suitable for JH or JL boxes only (not the earlier SH-type), a set of close-ratio gears cost £17 16s 6d — the actual ratios are listed in an Appendix. At the same time Jaguar decided to fit the lightened flywheel to all XK 120s (not just SE models), but

for some reason they began supplying XK 120 SE *fixed-heads* with single, not dual exhausts (from March 1953). On the subject of changes, the oil sump level element was deleted from the XK's specification in October 1952 (some time after the sports cars had adopted the Mark VII stepped sump during November 1951) and the racing screens and cowls which had apparently been supplied as standard with all Special Equipment XK 120 roadsters were only available from September 1953 to special order (judging by the scarcity today of original screens and cowls, it is hard to believe that all SE roadsters were dispatched from Coventry with these items on board).

XK 120 production came to a close in the autumn of 1954, and recalling the impact of the car worldwide, the comparatively small quantity of cars made comes as rather a surprise — 7,631 open-two-seaters, 2,678 fixed-heads, and just 1,769 drop-heads. Yet the XK 120 did a superb job for Jaguar — an afterthought car, an unplanned, incidental offshoot of the saloon range, it enhanced the Jaguar image enormously, besides earning many thousands of valuable dollars. It also proved that a twin-overhead-camshaft engine could be sold and serviced by ordinary garages all over the world and give six-figure mileages in the hands of normal drivers before overhaul. Furthermore, it demonstrated that an ultra-fast sports car need not be uncomfortable, or untractable in heavy traffic, or require any great measure of driving skill to achieve high point-to-point average speeds over all types of road. Finally, the XK 120 was one of the most beautiful sports cars Britain ever produced.

CHAPTER 3

The XK 140

1954 to 1957

The XK 140 showed that development of the XK series was to take the path of increasing refinement rather than out-and-out speed, for while the 'C-headed' XK 140s were undoubtedly quicker than their XK 120 predecessors, they were a little less crisp and certainly heavier. Visually, too, the car was less 'pure', but on the credit side the various alterations combined to make the XK 140 a considerably more practical and comfortable car to drive under everyday conditions.

The new model was announced at the 1954 motor show in October, and basically the three different types of body established by the XK 120 were retained. The standard XK 140 was powered by what had been the XK 120's 190-bhp SE unit, with the high-lift 3/8-inch cams, but with a single-pipe exhaust system; so far as the XK 140 was concerned Special Equipment now meant wire wheels and Lucas FT 576 foglamps. More power was available, though, in the form of the C-type head (readily identified by a cast 'C' in the plug well) which could be specified on SE models as an additional extra — an XK 140 thus equipped was rated at 210 bhp at 5,750 rpm on the twin 1¾-inch SU carburettors normally supplied (the bigger H2 items could still be ordered if desired). A dual exhaust system came with the 'C' head which, instead of the parallel-pipe layout of the XK 120 twin system, used two separate silencers with pipes which ran through holes in the chassis cross-member and emerged under each overrider at the rear of the car.

More important than these detail changes in layout was the fact that the position of the engine in the chassis had been altered; it now sat three inches nearer the front. The chief reason was almost certainly to provide room for a larger cockpit, as the front bulkhead could be moved forward a corresponding amount. But the change also affected the car's handling to a degree, and the additional weight on the front wheels (50.3 per cent instead of 47.5 per cent) enhanced the XK's already notable straightline stability at the expense of a little extra understeer on corners. The net result in practice was a car which could be driven at three-figure speeds in a hurricane without being noticeably deflected, and which felt even more stable on bends than the XK 120 — especially to less experienced drivers not used to tail-slides.

A second important change was the adoption of Alford and Alder rack-and-pinion steering on the XK 140; another example of racing improving the breed, this had previously been used with success on the C-type Jaguar, and thanks to less moving parts, gave a more direct response to the wheel. About the only disadvantage was a slight increase in kick-back (best dealt with by allowing the wheel to move slightly in the hands — it was always self-correcting), lessened soon after production began by a change in castor angle from 2½-3 degrees positive to 1½-2 degrees positive. The rack was secured to the frame by rubber-bonded mountings, which helped to cut down on vibrations as well.

The steering ratio remained at 2¾ turns lock to lock, although the turning circle was increased by a couple of feet (to 33 feet); a universally-jointed steering column was provided, which allowed the steering wheel to adopt a more comfortable angle in the car (as before, it was adjustable for reach after undoing a knurled ring). A new and more efficient radiator was installed at an angle to miss the rack, in conjunction with a new eight-bladed fan operating in a cowl.

The car's suspension had been subjected to only one change

The XK 140's engine bay, showing the new sloping radiator, and C-type head on this particular example.

The XK 140 fixed-head made a superb touring car, with plenty of room and a comparatively large glass area. This is a Special Equipment version with wire wheels and spotlamps.

The XK 140 drop-head in standard form, with pressed-steel wheels and no spotlamps. Note that the hub caps now have an all-chrome finish. Unlike the closed car, the drop-head had lever-type door handles.

The prototype XK 140 being evolved; the new bumpers are already in place and the new cast grille is being offered up. Lights remain XK 120 at this stage, the door handles are not yet push-button operated and the side-window pillar is slanting like the XK 120's.

At first, the XK 140 prototype carried an undivided rear bumper, with the numberplate being carried on the bootlid.

All the XK 140's rear-end details were new, including the lights, an exterior boot handle and a medallion recording Jaguar's Le Mans wins. The drop-head's rear window was no longer metal-framed, and was considerably larger than the XK 120's; it remained in a zipped panel.

that could be called major, and that was the substitution of Girling telescopic rear dampers for the previous lever-arm type. The upper ends of the new dampers were located on a bracket which triangulated the point where the rear chassis cross-member joined the chassis side-members just behind the rear axle; they operated on the rear axle via brackets attached to the axle casing, a little inboard of the more ideal point used by the earlier type, but in operation the new dampers were more efficient and certainly remained effective for much longer than the old. At the front, where telescopic dampers were already fitted, the XK 120's Special Equipment torsion-bars became standard, largely because of the new model's extra weight.

Little was changed when it came to the braking system, with the self-adjusting front brakes and the manual bevel-wheel rear brake adjustment being retained; but as few advantages had ensued from the use of a tandem master-cylinder, Jaguar went back to a single type for the XK 140, as used on earlier XK 120s. As before, wire-wheeled XK 140s had dished front brake drums which therefore were not interchangeable with the rears, and the 16 × 5K wheels had 54 spokes. The pressed wheels were again as for the later XK 120s, with 5½-inch rims, but the hub-caps now had an all-chrome finish, rather than being painted bodycolour in recessed areas.

Most of the changes which affected the appearance of the car were mainly due to the demands of the North American market, where the XK had proved so popular. In particular, the XK 120's rudimentary bumpers, mounted virtually directly on to the wings at the front, had proved incapable of warding-off parking assaults by American-made 2½-ton monsters, so they were replaced by much heavier Mark VII-pattern items. At the front these were carried on spring-steel bumper irons which passed through openings in the wings (which had originated as brake-cooling slots on the XK 120) and bolted directly to that massive chassis, the metalwork being neatly covered by a valance which ran between bumper and body. Quarter-bumpers were still used at the rear, but they were of similar section to the front and were mounted horizontally almost flush with the bodywork. Equally strong overriders were fitted front and rear, and the new bumper arrangements were responsible for adding some 3 inches to the XK's length, which was now up to 14 ft 8 in.

The car's appearance had also been altered by a new radiator grille; this was now a die-cast item with less numerous but thicker slats, which were integral with the surround. An enamelled badge was set into this surround, in place of the bonnet-mounted brass and 'ivory' badge of the XK 120, and the bonnet gained a centre chromium-plated strip (but no mascot). New Lucas J700 headlamps flanked the grille, and instantly noticeable were the large direction indicators set below.

At the rear, the flashing indicators were incorporated in much larger rearlight units as part of a complete rearrangement of the back end. As the new bumpers prevented any horizontal withdrawal of the spare wheel, this was now removed after lifting up a hinged lid (secured by budget locks) inside the luggage compartment. The bootlid itself no longer carried the numberplate (which was situated between the quarter-bumpers) but instead wore a new pushbutton handle, whose surround continued into an enamelled medallion proclaiming Jaguar's Le Mans wins. A chrome-plated centre strip completed the lid's decorations; like the bonnet, the lid itself was in aluminium.

These changes and additions were to be seen on all three body

Standard XK 140 fixed-head, with pressed-steel wheels and spats. Equipment on all XK 140s now included J700 headlamps (PF700 for the USA) and big flashing indicators set into the front wings.

styles, which did, however, retain the same basic wing line of the XK 120. But on the 'upper deck', the panelwork had been altered to accommodate the extra roominess which moving the engine now allowed. The fixed-head model in particular was now an extremely spacious sports car, for not only was advantage taken of the repositioned power unit, but the bulkhead and footwells were extended either side of the engine to enable the front seats to be brought forward almost one foot. The 6-volt batteries formerly behind the seats were transferred to compartments in the front wings and their place was taken by two occasional seats upholstered in plain leather — admittedly these could only accommodate children, or one adult sitting sideways, with any degree of comfort, but at least Dad no longer had to leave the family behind.

Also helping to create room for the new furnishings was the extension of the fixed-head's top 6¾ inches rearwards, and the revised windscreen position, which was now more forward. An additional 1½ inches of headroom was provided, and the larger windows which could now be fitted improved visibility and made the XK 140 less claustrophobic than its earlier counterpart. Wider doors (38-inch instead of 32½-inch) added to the general convenience of the car, which was now an express carriage

Very early XK 140 fixed-heads had occasional rear seats with full-length squabs, but this arrangement was soon discontinued.

suitable for any executive too young for a chauffeured Rolls-Royce.

The luxury image was encouraged by the car's interior trim, which again followed the pattern set by Jaguar saloons since before the war with its tasteful burred walnut veneer for dashboard, door and window pillar cappings — all made from 'real trees' in Jaguar's large saw mill and supplied to the trim line in sets with matching grain and colouring (in fact if you ordered spares, it was necessary to state whether a light or dark shade was needed). Instruments were similar to those of the XK 120's, but the dashboard now included a plated 'arrow-head' switch which operated the flashing indicators (it was self-cancelling, thanks to a clockwork time mechanism). For the new option of a Laycock de Normanville overdrive, an operating switch of mock cut-glass was positioned on the facia to the right of the steering column (on RHD cars) and it was internally illuminated when the overdrive was engaged.

The drop-head XK 140 also benefitted from the repositioned engine, and like the closed car it was a two-plus-two with similar occasional seats at the back in place of two 6-volt batteries — these had been exchanged for a single 12-volt battery, however, carried in the nearside front wing. The drop-head coupe's top resembled

This was the more normal rear-seating arrangement on XK 140 fixed-heads — ideal for children, if not adults. Above the seats, the rear bulkhead could be hinged down for direct access to the boot, which was also helpful for carrying very long objects.

The XK 140 drop-head in SE form; the soft top was beautifully made, although the wide corner panels of the top did not help visibility, especially if one was emerging at an angle from a side turning.

that of the earlier car's, beautifully made and very easy to erect; folded, it could be covered with a hood envelope which matched the exterior fabric.

The XK 140 open-two-seater, perhaps rather surprisingly, remained quite primitive in comparison with the luxurious coupes, for the roadster body style continued to lack wind-up windows, occasional rear seats or a fixed windscreen. It was therefore much more like a 'real' sports car than its two sisters — but that's what the majority of overseas customers wanted (particularly in North America), so that's what Jaguar gave them. To good effect, too, because while the XK 140 roadster is a rarity in Britain, more of this body style was built than any other type of XK 140.

Not that the two-seater failed to take any advantage of the mechanical rearrangements, for its bulkhead had been brought forward to give more space in the cockpit; this was used to allow an increase in seat travel of 3 inches. The scuttle line was also lifted an inch, which meant that the steering column could be

The superb walnut finish on the XK 140's dashboard. The steering wheel now had a safer boss, while the doors were opened by sliding knobs (visible just above the wheel spoke).

Inside the XK 140 drop-head there was not quite as much room as with the closed car, but the occasional seats were excellent for children.

raised to provide more clearance between the driver's thighs and the 18-inch steering wheel; the higher scuttle also provided better headroom when the hood was up.

As with the other cars, there were no longer any batteries behind the seats, but in the roadster, the space left was not used for additional seats, but instead served as extra luggage space (and as with all XK 140s, there was now access to the boot from inside the car, via a hinge-down board; this enabled objects 9 feet or more long to be carried, using boot and front passenger seat space — not bad for a sports car!). The 12-volt battery was fitted into the offside front wing space. Interior trim was much as before, except that upholstery, door trim panels and dashboard were all the same colour — no wood for the dashboard of course, which was now vertical instead of being mounted at an angle.

Most of the racing-type options which had been available to XK 120 roadster owners remained in the XK 140 catalogue, including bucket seats and aeroscreens. A competition clutch, and lead-bronze main and big-end bearings could also be ordered, along with 9:1 compression-ratio pistons — these mechanical items could also be specified on either of the two coupes.

A Special Equipment XK 140 with the C-type head was a very fast car indeed, no matter if weight had gone up by about 1 cwt (or a little more in the case of the drop-head); *The Autocar* achieved a resounding 129.6 mph mean speed during their road test of a fixed-head coupe. This was no fluke, either, because with the overdrive it was impossible to over-rev the engine with this very high (3.18:1) ratio engaged, and given a reasonable straight the car would just wind itself up and up; my own completely standard XK 140 drop-head with C-type head would reach an indicated one-way 138 mph under good conditions when 10 years old.

Of course this high ultimate speed was not used often, even by fast drivers, but the value of quoting it is to show how relaxed the car was at, say, 100 mph — which was reached extremely rapidly for such a fully-equipped two-plus-two at around 30 seconds. With the overdrive this speed represented an easy cruising gait, with the engine turning over at a mere 3,800 rpm. Acceleration

The XK 140 roadster's cockpit had no occasional seats, but instead contained a useful luggage space, lined with Hardura. Below the sidescreens' shelf, the bulkhead folded down to reveal the luggage boot (the rubber strakes were not standard).

A good view of the XK 140 roadster's rear-end details, showing the new 'swan neck' mounting for the familiar reversing/numberplate lamp, the push-button boot handle, the medallion and the chrome centre strip.

The XK 140 roadster retained most of the sporting characteristics of the XK 120, including detachable windscreen and hood with small rear window. This is an American-specification Special Equipment car.

A Jaguar XK 140 experiment. Chassis engineer R. J. (Bob) Knight — a future Jaguar managing director — tries out a roadster fitted with bonnet louvres, extra inlets (rather similar to the Le Mans 140's) and tufts of wool to delineate airflow.

was helped by the low (4.09:1) final-drive ratio which was provided when the overdrive was specified, and *The Autocar* found that their XK 140 reached 60 mph in 11 seconds — a figure which, I feel, does not altogether do justice to the XK's accelerative prowess because on the road it feels rather quicker, thanks to the torque of the engine, which gives such outstandingly good top-gear acceleration.

Due to its lighter weight, the XK 140 roadster was much quicker off the mark; it was never formally tested in Britain, but it went the rounds of the major journals in the United States, usually in 'MC' specification (Modified — SE — form, with C-type head). *Road & Track* tried a car fitted with the 3.54 axle of non-overdrive XK 140s, but still recorded a 0-60 mph time of 8.4 seconds, which is quick even by today's standards; the 'ton' arrived in 26½ seconds, and the mean maximum speed was 121.1 mph — indicating that the fixed-head probably had a 'cleaner' shape, and that overdrive was needed to obtain the best

results in this direction. Fuel consumption came out at between 16 and 18 mpg, which was modest in the circumstances — fast touring in an overdrive car could return 20 mpg or even better.

The XK 140 did not have quite the glamour of the XK 120, and additional weight, which put even more of a strain on those drum brakes, mitigated against a truly successful competition career. On the subject of brakes, in January 1958, after the car was technically obsolete, Jaguar offered a servo-assistance kit for the XK 140, but this was merely to provide lighter pedal pressures and did nothing to combat fade. The XK 140 also lacked the sophistication of its successor, the XK 150, and so has always played an 'in-between' role. However, brakes apart, some people actually prefer it to the XK 150, the bulkier lines and higher scuttle and doors of which can give the driver a feeling of always peering over something. Fewer XK 140s were made than any other type of XK, so owners can also boast that their car has something of a rarity-appeal!

CHAPTER 4

The XK 150 and XK SS

1957 to 1960

The arrival of the XK 150 in the spring of 1957 marked the biggest revision yet of the XK. It looked different inside and out, and at last the braking problem had been solved, for the latest version of Jaguar's sports car came with Dunlop disc brakes all round.

The new car was virtually sold on those brakes alone, and a drawing of the new equipment had pride of place in the centre page of the XK 150 brochure. 'The greatest technical advance of all', said the copy, '. . . immensely powerful yet smooth acting disc brakes on all four wheels bringing the power to stop, swiftly and surely, without the slightest loss of efficiency even after repeated applications from high speed'. And it was all largely true.

With the XK 150, Jaguar were the first manufacturer to offer four-wheel disc brakes on a genuine series-production car (as opposed to limited-edition special models). They had begun experiments with the new type of brake in 1951, and in conjunction with Dunlop they gradually overcame the many initial problems until, after an exploratory run at Reims, a C-type Jaguar equipped with disc brakes won the 1953 Le Mans race. In the meantime, production versions of the brake were undergoing lengthy tests on XK 120s (including the hard-worked HKV 455, the first XK built) until everyone considered that they were sufficiently developed to be incorporated into a true production Jaguar.

The big advantage of the disc brake, of course, is its heat-dissipating qualities — most of the friction area is open and exposed to the cooling air. Unlike that used on the competition C-types and D-types, the production disc brake used by Jaguar employed a single caliper containing one wheel cylinder on each side to grip the disc, instead of three each side. As no self-servo action was present, a form of assistance was virtually essential, and a Lockheed vacuum servo was incorporated, complete with a vacuum tank supplied by inlet-manifold pressure. An additional small caliper bridging the rear discs was for the fly-off handbrake, which needed fairly constant adjustment to maintain a reasonable degree of efficiency.

Theoretically, the new disc brakes were an optional extra, as a standard XK 150 was catalogued with Lockheed two-leading-shoe drum brakes, similar to those used on the XK 140, but it is almost certain that no XK 150s to this specification were produced for sale — Jaguar's advertising and publicity campaign, which so enthusiastically proclaimed the merits of the disc brake, effectively saw to that! Pressed-steel wheels were another seldom seen characteristic of the basic model, though unlike the drum brakes, a number of XK 150s were fitted with these, in which case the car was also equipped with rear-wheel spats.

Most XK 150s, therefore, were sold as Special Equipment models, with the familiar centre-lock wire wheels — at first usually with 54 spokes, although from June 1958 a stronger 60-spoke wheel was adopted; wheel diameter and rim width were always as for the XK 140. Engine capacity was still 3,442 cc and it was basically the 190-bhp XK 140 power unit; those who wanted more power could order what the factory termed a B-type cylinder-head. This had been developed mainly for the saloon cars and had the characteristic of giving the C-type head's 210-bhp rating, but at the lower rpm of 5,500. More importantly, the maximum torque of 216 lb ft was developed at 3,000 rpm,

1,000 rpm less than formerly, which meant a usefully better top-gear performance.

This had been achieved by keeping the larger exhaust valves of the C-type head, while retaining the smaller-diameter inlet throat of the standard (190-bhp) head, which kept the speed of the mixture up at a lower rpm. As a further aid to a more efficient gas-flow, the inlet valve angles were changed from 30 degrees to 45 degrees, and the valve faces were now convex instead of completely flat as before. The camshafts were left alone, as indeed they were to be for a good many years yet. Two 1¾-inch SU carburettors were still used, although they were bolted to a new inlet manifold, which had a separate water gallery on top (instead of being cast integrally). A single SU electric fuel pump still drew the petrol from the 14-gallon tank.

The drive-train followed XK 140 practice, with a short-shafted Moss gearbox worked by a stubby gear-lever, a Borg & Beck 10-inch diameter clutch, and the option of either an overdrive or an automatic Borg-Warner gearbox, similar to that fitted to the Mk VII saloon and a few late XK 140s. Although the automatic box was still a minority choice, about twice as many XK 150s as XK 140s left the factory with it. Final-drive gearing for overdrive-equipped cars was 4.09:1 as before, but standard and automatic cars were given the 3.54 ratio.

Apart from the glint of discs through the wire wheels, the mechanical changes incorporated in the XK 150 were not detectable from outside, although the bodywork alterations were very apparent. Even at the time they were a little controversial, and not everyone approved of the new high front wing line, which

This is what Jaguar shouted about when the XK 150 was launched — Dunlop disc brakes, the outcome of much experimentation on both road and track. This picture also shows clearly Jaguar's rack-and-pinion steering.

Ingenious facelift for the XK. Clever modifications to existing wings produced in the XK 150 a different-looking car without recourse to major retooling.

The rear of the XK 150 followed the XK 140 pattern; underneath the skin, the old XK chassis remained, but with the great added attraction of disc brakes.

XK 150s with pressed-steel wheels are very rare; as with all such XKs, the rear wheels were covered by spats. This is a late-model XK 150 with the larger rear light units incorporating an amber flasher lens (on home market cars).

Early XK 150s were equipped with a boot handle which ended short of the numberplate light cover. As can be seen in other pictures, on later cars it finished actually on the cover.

ran back to join the rear wing very close to its top, or the much wider grille, which much resembled that of the new 3.4 saloon. Also borrowed from the unitary-construction saloons was the styling for the XK 150's front bumpers; at the front, the formal straight line of the XK 140 bumper had been relieved by a dip in the bumper blade as it ran under the grille, while at the rear, the numberplate had been transferred to a moulding in the bootlid to allow the new wrap-round bumper blade to run the full width of the car. Then, for the first time on an XK, a 'leaping Jaguar' bonnet mascot was offered as an extra.

A distinctly modernizing feature of the XK 150 was its wrap-round windscreen of toughened glass, in place of the old-fashioned and inconvenient divided one (the little wipers did a poor job of clearing the glass) used on all previous XKs. Although this was not taken to the extremes which North American car makers, intrigued by the possibilities of curved glass, adopted at the time (the Vauxhall Victor and Cresta also exemplified the craze in Britain), it gave slightly better visibility, though some of the advantage was lost because it was installed on a higher scuttle. This meant that it was a shallower screen than on earlier XKs, a

What might have been . . . a totally new car to replace the XK 140, at least from the bodywork point of view. This mock-up has been assembled in front of Sir William's house at Wappenbury — he always viewed new designs against a 'real' (as opposed to a factory) background before making a final decision. A standard XK 140 provides a comparison.

The stillborn prototype (which was never a running car) looked particularly sleek from the rear. Other versions, with a larger and higher cockpit, were proposed as well.

factor which, along with the higher door line, was inclined to make the occupants of an XK 150 feel slightly buried.

The net result of these exterior changes was a car which to the Jaguar owner looked very different, yet one which someone with only a casual knowledge of the marque had great difficulty telling apart from an XK 140, unless the two were parked side-by-side. As *Road & Track* said at the time, 'it is easy to say that a little more should have been spent in order to introduce another sensation comparable to the first XK 120'.

The journal could not have known how nearly right it was — Sir William Lyons (he had been knighted in 1956) had indeed considered launching a totally rebodied car at this time, which borrowed nothing from previous XKs. Its streamlined shape anticipated later Jaguars in some of its features, and several different body layouts were proposed, including an open two-seater with wind-up windows, a two-plus-two coupe and a racy two-seater hardtop version. Sir William had all but finalized the styling of the new sports car when it was decided that it was beyond the resources of the factory at that time to tool-up for an entirely new bodyshell. So the XK 150 as we know it came into being.

But the XK 150 also had a new body, you might think. Not really so. Virtually no major retooling was necessary as the XK 150 body cunningly employed many of the existing XK 120/140 panels. For instance, the front wings, which made up most of the forward part, were based on the previous car's, the top portion of the wing simply being pivotted-up to provide the higher wing line, and the lower part altered to meet the door line.

The engine bay of an early (3.4) XK 150, with the B-type cylinder-head. There was a bit more room than in the XK 120, but not much!

The completely revised dashboard of the XK 150, leather-trimmed, with instrument panel in contrasting shade.

Early XK 150s had an XK 140-type direction indicator switch, tucked away under the facia roll; later cars had the more modern steering-column stalk control.

In this way the expensive tooling used to produce the curved parts of the wing could be left unaltered. Similarly, XK 120/140 bonnet pressings were still used, the extra width being introduced by a raised fillet added in the centre (a similar dodge was used by Alec Issigonis for the Morris Minor bonnet when, just before that car was released, he decided to widen it). So Jaguar produced a very acceptable 'new look' XK at a typically economic cost!

This new style was also very much in evidence inside the XK 150, where there was even more space, thanks to a 4-inch increase in width achieved by using thinner doors. For the first time in any production Jaguar, a padded facia roll was used, covered in leather, a material which was also employed for the instrument panel and the entire facia. The layout of the instruments themselves was much as before, with the starter still operated by a separate button. The driving mirror was now roof-mounted, taking advantage of the larger rear window, and the indicators were controlled from the top centre of the dashboard, although later XK 150s were to follow the trend towards stalk controls.

The seats looked much the same, but were slightly wider; they

The XK 150's occasional rear seats were a little wider than the XK 140's, but were still for emergency use only for adults.

bootlid. The method of closing the boot was not all that satisfactory, with a system of wires and catches being operated by the handle — if something broke you were in trouble! XK 150 door locks also proved somewhat fragile in use, and tended to wear out rather quickly. A locking petrol filler flap (opened by using the glove compartment key) was still used, and some cars were afflicted by an occasional smell of petrol inside the car when the tank was full.

The drop-head coupe followed the same pattern as its XK 140 forbear, so far as the top arrangements were concerned, the lined mohair hood giving a saloon-car air to the car when it was erected. But there was no roadster model in the XK 150 range when the new sports car was announced in May 1957, although it was on its way. As before, the cars represented amazing value for money, a Special Equipment XK 150 costing only £46 more than the equivalent XK 140 in those happy days before inflation.

Early XK 150s had a 'solid' armrest on the door, which was later modified to this shape, so that it could act as a door pull as well.

still lacked any sort of squab adjustment, however. Apparently, the company would still supply competition-type bucket seats, and some owners fitted the expensive and fully adjustable Reutter seats, which were catalogued as an extra for the Mk VIII saloon but not, it seems, for the XK 150. Large map pockets were contained in the doors, as well as pull-out ashtrays and arm-rests. As with previous XKs, no door checks of any sort were fitted, and it was all too easy for a gust of wind to catch the door and blow it wide open against the front wing, with consequent damage.

The XK 150's luggage compartment had about the same capacity as the XK 140's, quite shallow and with the spare wheel and jack being stored in a well, disclosed by lifting up the rear part of the boot floor. Some room was taken up by a tubular boot-lid prop, which was later discarded in favour of a spring-loaded

An XK 150 drop-head coupe in export trim accelerates along an English road. The dip in the front bumper softened the car's frontal appearance compared to the XK 140.

Like the XK 140, the XK 150's spare wheel lived in a well under the boot floor, with a lid released by a 'T' handle. Later cars had sprung bootlids which did away with the tubular prop shown here. *(Motor)*.

Automatic transmission cost an extra £192, overdrive £67, and a Radiomobile wireless set around £35.

Despite its extra weight and frontal area — the drop-head coupe was the heaviest XK ever to be made at 29½ cwt ready to go — the XK 150 performed surprisingly well, although Jaguar made sure that it was the Special Equipment version with the B-type head which was usually lent to the motoring press for road-testing. So when *The Autocar* tried a 210-bhp fixed-head coupe, early in 1958, there was an expected drop in top speed (from almost 130 mph to 123 mph in overdrive top), but an unexpected improvement in acceleration, 60 mph now being gained in a rapid 8.5 seconds as opposed to the XK 140's 11 seconds. Most of the credit must go to the B-type head, with its more useful torque curve, also reflected in the better top-gear acceleration figures. When it came to the old trick of starting off in top gear and accelerating to 100 mph, the later car managed the feat in 36.4 seconds, or 8.2 seconds quicker than when Harold Hastings and Joe Lowrey had tried the same thing with the original XK 120, almost 10 years before.

But inevitably, it was the disc brakes which made the biggest

For a two-seater sports car the XK 150 roadster was distinctly luxurious and came complete with wind-up windows and fully trimmed doors.

The XK 150 roadster looked surprisingly attractive with the hood erected; this is an export car, photographed at the factory.

impression on drivers in those days, and their efficiency and resistance to fade added immensely to the joy of driving such a fast car, because it was possible now to use all the performance without any fear about not being able to stop afterwards — something hard to appreciate today, with the almost universal use of disc brakes on even the humblest of family cars. The Jaguar XK, with its great power and not inconsiderable weight, had been very much in need of some drastic improvement to its stopping power.

The XK 150 range was completed in March 1958, when the open two-seater was announced from Coventry. While broadly similar in concept to the original XK roadsters, the XK 150 version was rather more civilized, having wind-up windows in the doors and a full, non-detachable windscreen — features which caused the more masochistic of enthusiasts to wince. But at least any attempt at two-plus-two seating had been avoided, and the XK 150 roadster was meant strictly for two — although in emergencies a child could be sat on the padded transmission tunnel between the wide, saloon-type seats.

Behind the seats there was now extra luggage space, and the

The 'S' engine with the straight-port head arrived as an option with the coming of the comparatively rare open-two-seater version of the XK 150. This is a left-hand-drive 3.4S with painted wire wheels.

This was the factory's 3.4S press car, as tested by *Motor* in 1959. The only outside identification of the 'S' engine is a discreet 'S' badge in chrome on the door.

rear tonneau panel was brought much further forward to end just short of the driver's and passenger's seat squabs, giving a very large rear 'deck' behind. The mohair single-thickness hood, easier to operate and better looking than previous Jaguar roadster tops, disappeared behind the seats as before, although this time the aperture between seats and rear deck was covered by a neat cover in hood material, which snapped in place over the top. Production was initially reserved for overseas (especially the United States, where the open-top body style was still so popular), and in fact very few roadster XK 150s remained in Britain.

Along with the XK 150 open two-seater came news of a new version of the XK engine. Part of Jaguar's search for more power during an escalating horsepower race in North America, the 'S' engine, as it was termed, used a reworked cylinder-head developed largely by Harry Weslake. This became known as the 'straight-port' head, a slight misnomer, but indicating the biggest change which had been made, namely the partial straightening of the ports, which was found to result in a better flow of mixture at high rpm.

To allow full advantage to be taken of the improved breathing, three 2-inch carburettors were fitted on an entirely new inlet manifold consisting of three sections, each carburettor feeding two tracts, which then separated and led direct to one inlet port; the tracts were curved to produce an equal length from each carburettor to each port, thus ensuring a uniform ram effect. The carburettors were fitted with air trumpets of optimum length, each breathing through a steel-mesh air filter contained in a Cooper air-box. Additionally, 9:1-compression pistons were standardized for the 'S' engine, as were lead-bronze bearings, a lightened flywheel and a stronger clutch assembly. The total effect was to increase the rating from 210 bhp to 250 bhp at 5,500 rpm, the torque figure rising from 216 lb ft to 240 lb ft at 4,500 rpm (1,500 rpm higher than before). Twin SU electric fuel pumps provided the extra flow of petrol needed at high engine revolutions.

At first the new engine was only supplied in the roadster, and it made an already fast car an exceptionally rapid one. *Road & Track* compared the times returned by a standard XK 150 roadster and a 3.4 'S' version, and found that the more powerful

A try-out of a cutaway spat for the wire-wheeled XK 150; it did little for the car's looks and not surprisingly it was never introduced into the range.

Coachbuilders turned their attention to the XK series from time to time and a practical and very well executed example was this British conversion of an XK 150 to an estate; the car was owned by Douglas Hull.

The XK 150's engine bay was rather full, especially when the triple-carburettor 'S' engine was installed; note the air filter inside the wing.

car reached 60 mph in 7.3 seconds (1.6 seconds quicker) and covered the standing quarter-mile in 15.1 seconds (1.7 seconds faster). Maximum speed in overdrive was 136 mph, the best yet recorded for an XK model.

About the only change to the rest of the car was an alteration to the brakes, although this was not aimed so much at an improvement in efficiency, but rather in convenience. Originally it had been necessary to dismantle the brake wheel cylinders to change the pads, which meant bleeding the system; now, the redesign allowed the new square-shaped pads to be changed in minutes after simply withdrawing a clip. This much more satisfactory method was soon adopted for all Jaguars.

Towards the end of 1958, the XK 150 open two-seater became available on the home market, and by the spring of 1959 the 'S' engine could be supplied with any of the XK 150 body styles. *The Motor* soon found that the XK 150S fixed-head coupe returned a

very similar performance to that of the racing C-type Jaguar of only a few years previously, 60 mph being reached in 7.8 seconds, and 100 mph in 20.3 seconds; maximum speed was 132 mph, while no particular penalty was extracted by way of fuel consumption, which was a modest 18.6 mpg overall.

To help get the car off the line, and to minimize wheelspin caused by weight transference on corners, the XK 150S could now be supplied with a Thornton Powr-Lok differential, which used a system of clutches to limit the slip of the least-loaded wheel. This it did quite efficiently, although it tended to wear out after a few thousand miles in the hands of a fast driver. However, it did not overcome the fact that the XK's rear suspension was now becoming dated, especially in comparison with the more advanced continental sporting cars. This was particularly the case with the extra power of the 'S' engine, and axle tramp caused by spring wind-up often occurred when the car was accelerated hard

The D-type Jaguar, which formed the basis for the XK SS; 'Lofty' England, wearing the blazer, organizes the Jaguar team at Reims prior to the 12-hours race in 1956, when they finished first, second and third.

out of a second-gear corner, or when the clutch was dropped for a rapid take-off from rest.

In other respects, the XK's chassis had stood up well to the extra power and weight that it had accumulated since 1948, and it still provided handling and ride qualities which were rated good by the standards of the late-'fifties. John Bolster summed it up well by saying that the XK 150, 'may not have the extreme cornering power of some more radical designs . . . but it scores by giving the driver plenty of warning that the limit is being approached. For this reason the XK 150S is a particularly safe sports car'. As with previous XKs, the XK 150's handling became a lot crisper if the tyre pressures were raised about 10 psi, which cut out most of the squeal and gave the car a more precise feel at speed.

But those who had noted that the Mark IX Jaguar saloon shown at the October 1958 motor show boasted a larger, 3,781-cc version of the XK engine must have guessed that a potentially even faster

XK 150 was in the offing, and sure enough, when the factory released news of the 1960 range, 3.8-litre XK 150s were included. The new capacity could be specified in any of the three body styles, and in either normal or 'S' form. This gave the customer a wide range of engine options — standard or 'S' 3.4, and standard or 'S' 3.8, plus a choice of compression ratios (7:1, 8:1 and 9:1) which further affected power output. He could also choose between manual, manual-plus-overdrive, or automatic transmission — though not on the 'S' models, which came with overdrive as standard.

The capacity of 3.8 litres had been associated with the XK engine for some years, Oscar Moore in Britain and Phil Hill, amongst others, in the United States having experimented with over-bored engines since the early-'fifties. But Jaguar's own 3.8-litre engine used cylinder liners to accommodate the larger bores (up from 83 mm to 87 mm) from which was derived the extra capacity, as simply boring the existing block was inclined to

The D-type's construction was vastly different from that of the XK road cars, with a centre tub supporting a forward framework which took the engine; the rear wheels are cantilevered from the rear bulkhead.

The XK SS, which was pure D-type except for the windscreen, weather equipment, luggage rack and more complete cockpit trim.

produce cracking between the cylinders. With the B-type head, the 3.8-litre engine was rated at 220 bhp and with the straight-port head and triple 2-inch SU HD8 carburettors the figure was an extremely healthy 265 bhp.

Not that the XK 150 was the principal reason for Jaguar developing this most powerful (until then) production version of the XK engine. Its ultimate home was intended to be the new range of independent-rear-suspension sports and saloon cars which were just around the corner, and indeed, had the E-type Jaguar been on schedule, it is possible that there would not have been a 3.8 XK 150S at all.

But there was, and a very rapid car it turned out to be, too. John Bolster was one of the few people to record figures during the model's relatively brief lifespan, his test being published in *Autosport* on June 17, 1960. Perhaps the most impressive of the figures captured by Bolster's stopwatch was the 0-100 mph time; at exactly 19 seconds it would very nearly match the figures to be obtained from production examples of the E-type Jaguar, then less than a year away, thanks in part to the low (4.09) final-drive ratio with which all overdrive-equipped XKs were provided.

There was no space for luggage in the bodywork of the XK SS, hence the rack, nor could the hood be folded down anywhere but on top of the rear deck, where it was covered by an envelope.

More trim, but still very workmanlike — the cockpit of the XK SS.

By the time 110 mph was reached, the 3.8 XK 150S was really striding away, the 22.2 seconds required being 3.4 seconds less than that taken by *The Motor's* 3.4S and, considered Bolster, it was in these higher speed ranges that the extra capacity really told, the acceleration from 100 to 120 mph not being noticeably less brisk than that from 80 mph to 100 mph. Maximum speeds in the gears were found to be 32, 60, 92 and (in direct top gear) 115 mph, while in overdrive (which operated on top gear only on all Jaguars), 136.3 mph was obtained. The XK 150S in 3.8-litre form was undoubtedly one of the world's fastest cars in its time, and for a considerable while after — even today, not many production cars of any description can achieve 100 mph in less than 20 seconds. Bolster must have enjoyed himself with YHP 791, because he recorded an all-time high for petrol consumption during a contemporary XK road test — 13 mpg!

Nor was the performance let down by the behaviour of the chassis or brakes — during fast driving, Bolster found the latter to be virtually faultless, although the handbrake was less satisfactory. High-speed motoring, despite a deliberate attempt to seek out bends with bumps and changes of camber, proved once again the XK's great virtue of unruffled stability, which John Bolster thought was even better than on previous XK models. As for cornering ability, Bolster saw the car as competent rather than exemplary, cornering very well, 'having regard to its substantial construction and conventional chassis design'. The 3.8-litre engine provided quite enough power to drift the car, 'even on very fast curves', although generally, Bolster felt that the XK 150S was best treated as a very fast touring car, rather than a 'tamed-down racing car'.

This was fair comment about a car which started life with essentially a saloon car chassis and which weighed some 4 or 5 cwt *more* than a five/six-seater Ford Zephyr. There was not much finesse in the handling of an XK 150, but it was entirely safe and few cars were capable of leaving it behind, no matter what the road. Nothing, of course, matched the XK 150 on a performance-for-money basis, as a glance at 1960 price lists will show. The most expensive XK was the 3.8S drop-head coupe at £2,204 — the closed Aston Martin DB4, which could barely match its performance, was £3,755; the Jensen 541R, which was considerably slower, cost £2,706; while the cheapest Ferrari, with just about the same acceleration, but considerably better

A full, dry-sump, D-type engine gave the XK SS a performance that is breathtaking even today — 100 mph could be achieved in around 13 seconds.

handling, was £5,951. There was also a good chance that the Jaguar would be longer-lasting (door locks apart!) and more reliable than any of the others.

Then, in March 1961, came the E-type, which made its debut at the Geneva motor show and created a similar furore to that which surrounded the XK 120 back in 1948. It made the XK 150 look old-fashioned and clumsy — but not ugly. A revelation though the E-type may have been, the XK range — particularly the last examples of the breed — could still score over its successor, which lacked the spaciousness of the XK 150 and, unless an optional high-ratio final-drive was specifically requested, was denied the lazy high-speed cruising associated with the XK's overdrive.

The XK 150 was Jaguar's last chassis-built sports car, and indeed it represented Jaguar's last-but-one sports car of all, if you count the later six-cylinder and V12 E-types as a single variety.

Like the XK 120 and XK 140 before it, the XK 150 was a very British motor car, suave, traditional and with a heart of gold — the magnificent XK engine. The XK Jaguars had their faults, but they are generally remembered with affection by their owners, most of whom fondly recall the enchantment of a fast drive on a warm summer's evening, accompanied by the distinctive, musical howl of that beautiful straight-six engine running up through the gears. On a good day there was almost nothing to beat it.

The XK SS

While it may have been called 'XK SS', in reality this car came from an entirely different branch of the Jaguar family tree to that of the XK series proper. It owed its existence to the number of racing D-type Jaguars which the company had to build to meet certain sports car regulations — not all of these 'production' D-types were sold (or even completed), so the idea of using them up to create an exciting road-going version of the sports-racing car seemed attractive, particularly as it appeared that the car would fit into the Sports Car Club of America's production sports car racing category.

The credit for producing the first road-equipped D-type must go to works driver Duncan Hamilton, though, who fitted OKV 1 (his ex-works 1954 Le Mans team car) with a windscreen and hood during 1956. Construction of the 'official' version began in the winter of 1956, and as with OKV 1, no structural alterations were made to the D-type's monocoque hull — the division between driver and passenger was removed, a door was installed on the nearside, and a large full-width windscreen, with a pronounced wrap-round, was placed on top of the scuttle. Its chromium-plated side pillars were integrated into the bodywork through an extra aluminium panel in body colour, which was also fixed to the scuttle. Small quarter-bumpers (more for effect than serious protection) were fitted on each corner of the body, and the side-mounted exhaust and silencer were shielded by a drilled, plated cover.

Weather protection was provided by a mohair hood, which folded down on to the rear tonneau panel behind the driver and passenger, to be covered by an envelope; detachable sidescreens with plated frames were also provided. The interior of the car was trimmed in leather, but room was restricted inside, and as there was no boot, luggage had to be carried on a rack mounted on the tail! Virtually no changes were made to the dry-sump 3.4-litre D-type engine, with its triple Weber carburettors, though a larger pulley could be fitted to increase the dynamo's charging rate for non-racing use.

Just 18 cwt and 250 genuine bhp (as opposed to the 3.8 XK 150S's true installed output of around 200 bhp) combined to produce a staggering performance for 1957, *Road & Track* magazine finding that the car returned figures of 5.2 seconds and 13.6 seconds for the 0-60 and 0-100 mph times, respectively — which few 'supercars' can match even today! The standing quarter-mile was covered in 14.1 seconds, and while the top speed was not recorded, it must have been in the region of 145-150 mph. As others discovered, there were practical drawbacks in using an XK SS for road work, such as an uncomfortable amount of heat from the exhaust on the passenger's side, but the ride was found to be notably smooth for what was still essentially a sports-racing car, and the windscreen made goggles unnecessary.

A mere 16 examples of the XK SS were built during the brief production run from late-1956 to early-1957 — it proved to be less suitable than was hoped in SCCA racing (though it did score some wins, the first being at Mansfield, Louisiana, in the spring of 1957, driven by C. Gordon Bennet), and maybe the price of £3,878, cheap though it was by absolute standards, limited the number of potential customers. A final halt to the building of the XK SS came in February 1957, when some of the remaining D-type shells were destroyed in Jaguar's famous fire — it was certainly not worth building more just for the XK SS. So it became one of the rarest Jaguars ever built, and remains to this day the fastest *catalogued* Jaguar sports car ever made.

CHAPTER 5

XKs in competition

Racing, rallying and record-breaking

By no means was the XK 120 designed with any thoughts of competition in mind, nor indeed was the new XK engine which powered it — although it needed little foresight to realize that when the two were combined, the machine which resulted must certainly have a potential on the track on the basis of its power/weight ratio alone. So when, in 1949, the BRDC and the *Daily Express* decided to hold a race at Silverstone for standard production cars, the XK 120 appeared to be a 'natural'.

Not that William Lyons was in any way blasé about the new sports car's chances in the race, even if on paper it appeared to be a reasonably certain winner. He therefore instructed that an XK 120 be driven to the proposed venue, the ex-bomber airfield at Silverstone, Northants (only 40 miles from the factory), which had recently been turned into a motor racing circuit, and 'flogged round for three hours' as 'Lofty' England expressed it later, to see if the car really was fast enough and reliable enough to win the event. England, Hassan and Rankin did most of the testing, but Lyons himself put in a good few laps, driving with his usual determination — indeed, as his occasional excursions in SS 100s before the war had demonstrated, Jaguar's managing director would have been a highly competitive driver had he chosen motor sport as a hobby!

On race day, all went well; ERA drivers Prince 'Bira' and Peter Walker and 328 BMW exponent Leslie Johnson conducted the three XK 120s which were entered. The story of the race has been told many times, and of course Leslie Johnson won in HKV 500 after 'Bira' spun off with a burst rear tyre after two-thirds of the hour-long race had been run. If the Prince had thought to drive the car on its flat tyre just a few yards to the concrete of one of Silverstone's many runways, where the jack would not have sunk into the soft earth, he could have changed the wheel successfully and secured Jaguar the team prize as well, which instead fell to the Healey team of Rolt, Chiron and Wisdom.

Nevertheless, that one-two victory at Silverstone began a tradition of Jaguar wins at that circuit, and also set the XK 120 on a racing career which, despite being far from the minds of its original designers, was to bring the company useful publicity and prestige and ultimately would result in the building of the C-type and D-type sports-racing cars, through whose wins at Le Mans the name of Jaguar was to be so firmly established throughout the world.

The XK's competition debut in the United States came in January 1950, when Leslie Johnson travelled to Palm Beach to drive an XK 120 against an assortment of American specials and another two XKs. A creditable fourth place and second in class was secured, the winner being George Huntoon in a Ford-Mercury V8-engined ex-Indianapolis Duesenberg! Second was Briggs Cunningham in a Cadillac-engined Healey; soon to become Jaguar's greatest American enthusiast, Cunningham had just bought an XK 120 himself (in pastel blue, Chassis Number 670023). As for the first XK win overseas, Andrew Whyte records Alfonso Gomez Mena's first place in the unlimited production car race of February 24, 1950, on the island of Cuba (his car, incidentally, was 670030, which had been dispatched to Jaguar's Havana agent, Frank Seiglie, in December 1949). In the United States, it was Phil Hill who gained the first XK 120 victory, at Pebble Beach, in November 1950.

Back in Britain, the Silverstone result had been sufficiently

August 1949, and the XK 120s are ready for the one-hour production car race at Silverstone. In the foreground is Leslie Johnson in the winning car. Some 100,000 people — over three times the number ever seen at any Brooklands meeting — watched him average 82.80 mph to take the chequered flag. Behind, Peter Walker gets into 670001 which, like HKV 500, had been converted to right-hand drive.

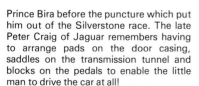

Prince Bira before the puncture which put him out of the Silverstone race. The late Peter Craig of Jaguar remembers having to arrange pads on the door casing, saddles on the transmission tunnel and blocks on the pedals to enable the little man to drive the car at all!

encouraging for Jaguar to prepare five XK 120s for private entrants to drive in various important racing events; one each went to Leslie Johnson and Peter Walker who had contributed to that initial Silverstone result, a third to motor trader Nick Haines, and another to driver-journalist Tommy Wisdom. The last car was the only one not sold, but lent, and it was delivered to the veteran Italian racing driver Clemente Biondetti. A sixth car was reserved for another type of motor sport — rallying — and Ian Appleyard was the recipient.

This was in the spring of 1950, and Biondetti's car (660043) was the first in action, tackling the Targa Florio in April; the XK 120 even led at one stage, ahead of Ascari's V12 Ferrari, but a rare broken connecting-rod put the Jaguar out of the running well before the finish — at least it had the effect of causing Jaguar to crack-test every rod used in their engines from then on, which meant that the limited racing programme was already producing data which could usefully be applied to the production cars.

Three weeks later, Biondetti, Johnson, Haines and Wisdom lined-up for the Mille Miglia. That often devastating race over a thousand miles of ordinary Italian roads was made all the more hazardous in 1950 by the streaming wet weather, and Haines crashed some 200 miles into the event. Biondetti, who had won the race with his Type 166 Ferrari in 1948 and 1949, lost 40 minutes early on through breaking a rear spring, thanks to the multitude of potholes and hump-backed bridges on the route. Tommy Wisdom had even worse luck, transmission problems halting him just 40 miles from the end, so it was left to Leslie Johnson, in JWK 651, to be classed as the only XK finisher. In fact he gained fifth place overall, a superb achievement in the circumstances as the very standard XK, designed purely as a road car, was in the main competing against such as the purpose-built 3.3-litre Ferraris.

The dual character of the XK 120 was underlined when Tommy Wisdom drove JWK 988 1,200 miles across Europe to run in the Circuit of Oporto, gaining third place behind an Alfa Romeo driven by Bonetto and an OSCA piloted by Carini. Wisdom then took the wheel of a Jowett Jupiter for 'the big one' of 1950, which was, of course, Le Mans.

It was a bold move, entering the 24-hours race with three XK 120s — but Jaguar had no illusions about their chances of a

Accelerating hard, JWK 651 squats down on its rear suspension as Leslie Johnson shows how competitive even a standard XK 120 could be at Le Mans; at one stage he was running in third place during the 1950 event.

Service for the Clark/Haines car during a pit stop at Le Mans in 1950; note the box of spares on the passenger's side and the French scrutineer with a bunch of seals ready to seal the oil and petrol filler caps.

The Le Mans XK 120s really were very standard — the flip-top oil-filler cap and wadding to ensure all the air from the grille went through the radiator are the only non-standard features to be seen in this underbonnet view of car number 16.

The Walker/Marshall car completes the 24-hours in 15th place — unlike JWK 651, which can just be seen at the side of the road after its clutch had expired a few hours before the finish.

win, and regarded the exercise as purely exploratory. As usual, the cars were entered under their drivers' names, in this case Leslie Johnson/Bert Hadley with JWK 651, Nick Haines/Peter Clark with the unregistered car with Chassis Number 660041 and Peter Walker/John Marshall in the former's JWK 977.

It has been alleged that these XK 120s were highly modified and not representative of production XKs, but nothing could be further from the truth. As Bill Heynes said, 'they were probably the most standard cars that have ever been run in this race'. For a start they weighed-in at over 30 cwt ready to go (the 'list' dry weight of the aluminium-bodied XK 120s was an optimistic 22 cwt, so Jaguar could have lightened the cars considerably had they wished), and their speed down the Mulsanne Straight was no faster than that achieved by Sutton at Jabbeke — or about par for a standard, carefully assembled XK 120.

The three cars ran with aeroscreens and cowled mirrors but not, it seems, undershields. The normal 14-gallon tank was replaced by a 24-gallon item, and spare parts and tools (the rules said that everything replaced must have been carried on the car itself) were contained in a box on the passenger's side as there was no room in the boot. Two big Lucas spotlights supplemented the headlights for night driving, and a quick-action filler cap was substituted for the normal locking flap.

Leslie Johnson and JWK 651 were nominated as the 'hare', with speed rather than any conservation of the car's mechanical parts being the main aim. But it was known well beforehand that trouble was most likely to stem from the XK's brakes, particularly as a wire-wheel conversion — which allowed a great deal more air to circulate and cool the overworked drums — was not yet available. Instead, heat dissipation was aided by a strange, turbine-like finned disc sandwiched between wheel and drum, the idea being that the disc would act like a fan and help cool the drum, which had holes drilled in its outer face.

It was not very effective, and although Johnson and Hadley had achieved third position by the early hours of the morning, vigorous use of the gearbox was necessary to slow the XK for corners. Despite this handicap, Johnson put in a lap of 96.98 mph shortly after midday on the Sunday, and had averaged almost 94 mph; this meant that the white XK 120 was gaining on Rosier's leading Talbot at a rate which meant that theoretically

The flying Stirling Moss tears past T. Flack's MG TD on the way to his 1950 TT win at Dundrod; his last lap was his fastest, incidentally!

the Jaguar actually had a chance of winning.

Then, at five minutes past one, the XK coasted to a halt within sight of the pits — JWK 651's run was over, the centre having pulled out of the clutch driven-plate following the strenuous use of the gearbox in lieu of brakes. The remaining two XKs easily lasted the 24 hours, however, and finished in 12th and 15th places, the Clark/Haines car in 12th position having averaged almost 81 mph, despite oil on the clutch, and covered 230 laps of the circuit to the winning Talbot's 256. If it was a defeat, it was an honourable one, and above all it proved to engineer Heynes, watching from the pits with Lyons and England, that gimmickry or years of practice were not necessary to produce a potential Le Mans winner — simply a good car with the necessary speed and stamina. The outcome, of course, was the all-conquering XK 120C, or C-type Jaguar, which used many of the XK 120's parts and was to be victorious at Le Mans both the next year and in 1953.

Meanwhile, the XK 120's rally career was about to begin, as Ian Appleyard embarked a few weeks afterwards on the 1950 Alpine Rally. The former SS 100 driver, now with his new bride, the former Pat Lyons, navigating, conducted NUB 120 over the road section with no loss of marks, despite the time taken by each car to *descend* a pass being added to the time recorded on the way up, which put a severe strain on those brakes, which still had to be manually adjusted — and that needed doing at virtually every control. The penalty-free run was maintained until the end of the rally, with the XK making fastest time over the flying kilometre (109.8 mph) and in the driving tests. The net result was a *Coupe des Alpes* and the equivalent of an overall win.

The next important track event of 1950 was the second *Daily Express*-sponsored International Trophy meeting at Silverstone, with production car racing again featuring in the programme. This time Walker was the victor, JWK 977 leading the similar car of Tony Rolt to the flag; Tazio Nuvolari had tried an XK 120 in

Jaguar's chief engineer William Heynes with Leslie Johnson and the faithful JWK 651 after averaging over 131 mph for an hour at Montlhéry.

the first practice session (his time was identical to Tommy Wisdom's), but he was far from well and did not take part in the race. Shortly afterwards, Peter Walker took his XK to the old-established hill-climb venue of Shelsley Walsh, gaining a class win in the over-3-litre production car class.

But the most significant racing event for Jaguar after Le Mans was the Tourist Trophy held at Dundrod, in Ulster, amid torrential downpours. Stirling Moss, just making a name for himself in 500-cc racing, managed to do a deal with Tommy Wisdom to borrow JWK 988, splitting expenses and any winnings. Not only did he put up the fastest practice lap, but the young Moss (who was 21 the day after the race) completed the 225 miles ahead of all comers to bring Jaguar their first really important long-distance racing victory, while Peter Whitehead and Leslie Johnson helped Jaguar to secure the team prize. The TT represented a personal landmark for Moss, too, because Lyons signed him up on the spot as a works driver — his first truly professional contract.

The first task assigned to him in his new role was to partner Johnson at Montlhéry, where JWK 651 proceeded to motor for 24 hours at an average speed of 107.46 mph, covering 2,579.16 miles in the process. The fastest lap put in was at 126.2 mph, and this was much improved upon when, in March 1951, five months later, the car returned to France and recorded one hour at 131.83 mph average, the fastest lap being at 134.43 mph — Bill Heynes, it seems, was trying out one of the new C-type heads prior to its use on the still-secret competition car!

The year 1951 was to be the XK 120's greatest in competition, the first big success being the Appleyards' first place in the Tulip Rally; the runner-up was the Swiss driver Habisreutinger in another (but steel-bodied) XK 120, who was to notch up many useful successes for Jaguar on the Continent. The Rallye du Soliel, the Scottish and RAC Rallies, and the International Alpine Rally also saw XK 120s in winning form. But perhaps most noteworthy of all was the victory by the Belgians Johnny Claes and Jacques Ickx in the Liège-Rome-Liège of August 1950, then rated the toughest rally in the calendar; they borrowed HKV 500, and the drive also brought Claes the Belgian National Trophy of Merit, the country's highest award for a sporting achievement.

The XK 120's performances on the track during 1951 more

One of the most successful XK 120 rallyists was Ruef Habisreutinger, from Switzerland, seen here on his way to a *Coupe des Alpes* in the 1951 event.

than supported the efforts of the rally drivers; Johnny Claes won the production sports car race on his home circuit at Spa, while Stirling Moss continued the Jaguar tradition of winning the *Daily Express* production car event at Silverstone, using JWK 675 (the first left-hand-drive steel-bodied XK 120, road-tested by *The*

Autocar before being converted to right-hand drive). Genuine private owners of note were also beginning to emerge, Duncan Hamilton and Hugh Howorth both winning at the airfield circuit of Boreham with their self-prepared XK 120s, while two or three Scotsmen were doing particularly well at Winfield and Turnberry.

It was not all success for the XK 120, though; Leslie Johnson and Stirling Moss each took a car on the 1951 Mille Miglia and failed to finish, mainly through the old problem with the brakes, while at Le Mans, private entrant Bob Lawrie's remarkable 11th place with his steel-bodied and very standard XK 120 was rather overshadowed by the C-type's magnificent overall win. However, the XK 120 does officially come into the 1951 Le Mans picture by proxy, because three special lightweight bodies were built for use on more-or-less production XK 120 chassis as a precaution should the C-types not have been ready in time.

Of course, they duly appeared on time, and the special bodies were put on one side without, it seems, having met a chassis.

Johnny Claes' and Jacques Ickx's famous victory in the 1951 'Liège'; alas, the hard-worked HKV 500 does not survive today, having been broken up by the factory during the 1950s.

Stirling Moss driving to first place in the 1951 Silverstone production car race with the first steel-bodied XK 120; chasing him is George Wicken in another XK 120.

Hugh Howorth leads Duncan Hamilton on the Boreham airfield circuit in 1951; later, Howorth purchased JWK 977, but this is his first XK.

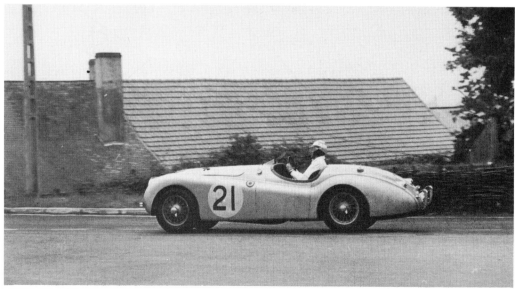

Bob Laurie's splendid drive with Ian Waller in AEN 546, which resulted in 11th place at Le Mans in 1951.

LT-3 as it is today, awaiting restoration by owner Tom Hendricks, but amazingly original; note the special features like the 'short' doors and one-piece rear body. (Tom Hendricks)

Unlike normal XK 120s, the Le Mans cars had a one-piece front-end and a lift-out bonnet section. The engine sports period 2-inch carburettors and sits behind a special radiator. (Tom Hendricks)

Their eventual fate might well have been the scrapheap, except that Charles Hornburg, Jaguar's West Coast distributor in the United States, spotted them during a trip to Coventry and arranged to buy two of them. They were shipped to America, mounted on new, standard XK 120 chassis taken straight from the line, and equipped with engines in approximately 'production C-type' state of tune, with two 2-inch carburettors. The body panels *were* special, the rear half of the car, including wings, being in one piece, and the bonnet being integral with the front wings, access to the engine being via a lift-out panel on top. Normal XK 120 doors were fitted, but they extended down only to the sill line. An absolute minimum of internal panelling was used, and the body was supported on a simplified type of 'superleggera' framework of small-diameter steel tubing.

These two unique XK 120s (dubbed 'Silverstones' in the USA) had a very reasonable measure of success in North American sports car events, racing initially for Hornburg as a team with none other than Phil Hill driving LT-3 (the bodies were numbered LT-1, 2 and 3 by the factory) against Ferrari, Cadillac-Allard and Cunningham opposition. Various drivers tried their hand with LT-2, Bill Breeze crashing it at Reno. LT-3's last national appearance was in the 1952 Watkins Glen Grand Prix meeting, after which it was sold to a St Louisville dealer — it survives to this day, as does the LT-2, which had acquired a new front-end (modelled on the C-type) by the mid-'fifties.

In Britain, the remaining bodyshell was rescued by Bob Berry, who was working in Bill Rankin's publicity office at Brown's Lane. This body was installed on his own XK 120 chassis (registered MWK 120) for the 1954 season, and careful development ensured that LT-1 became the fastest of the special XK 120 bodies, and was quite capable of beating the slower C-types. It ended-up with a full D-type engine, complete with Weber carburettors, before Bob Berry began racing Jack Broadhead's D-type Jaguar in 1955. A later owner, David Cottingham, raced MWK 120 in club events during the late-'sixties and recorded the rapid standing quarter-mile time of 13.3 seconds at the Santa Pod drag strip in Northamptonshire — barely a second slower than a production D-type could manage. The car resides in Canada at the time of writing.

For important track events, the XK 120 had been superceded

Inside the rear-end of LT-2, showing the light tubular frame on which the body of the Le Mans XK 120 was mounted.

LT-2 as it has ended up, back in Britain and being restored.

Hugh Howorth, one of the quickest of private entrants in XK 120s, driving JWK 977 with its C-type rear suspension conversion at Silverstone in 1953, chased by Oscar Moore's Jaguar-engined HWM. *(Harold Barker)*

Ecurie Ecosse began their Jaguar racing career with XK 120s — this is Sir James Scott-Douglas on the Isle of Man circuit during the 1952 British Empire Trophy race.

by the C-type by 1952 so far as Jaguar themselves were concerned, and five of the six works XK 120s passed into other hands. Some were to perform well for years in club racing, JWK 977 being fitted with a C-type rear-end for Hugh Howorth, and JWK 650 (the ex-Biondetti car, though minus its original engine, which the Italian driver used in a sports-racing car of his own design) making some impressively fast appearances in the hands of Harvey Baillie until the mid-'sixties. Pleasant to relate, all the works XKs survive in excellent order and with continuing racing histories to this day.

The sixth works-backed XK was kept very much in the fray, however. This, of course, was NUB 120, and suitably updated with wire wheels, self-adjusting front brakes and more horsepower, the white XK achieved its hat-trick of Alpine Rally performances in 1952, Ian Appleyard becoming the first man to complete three Alpines with no penalty points, a feat which gained him the first Alpine Gold Cup to be awarded. Many other fine rally performances were put up by private entrants with

XK 120s during 1952 and 1953, including Moss with his XK 120 fixed-head coupe, and it was during 1952 that Moss won his last race in an XK 120, leading home seven other identical XK roadsters at Silverstone during a Race of Champions at Silverstone.

The same year also saw the formation of Ecurie Ecosse, for whom David Murray, Sir James Scott-Douglas, Ian Stewart and Arthur Dobson all drove XK 120 roadsters. Murray retired from driving to manage the team, which soon passed on to C-types, then D-types and the ultimate achievement of two Le Mans wins. Far too many individual drivers scored minor successes with XK 120s during the mid- and late-'fifties to name them all here, though Dick Protheroe's success in the 1959 *Autosport* championship with his aluminium-bodied roadster GPN 635 should be mentioned, while Jackie Stewart won a race in an XK 120 as late as 1964 at a Jaguar Driver's Club meeting at Crystal Palace.

Although not exactly racing, two speed runs by Jaguars should

Fixed-head XK 120s were used as competition cars, too — this is Jack Sears in a determined mood during the Blackpool driving tests on the 1954 RAC Rally.

Ian Appleyard retired NUB 120 for 1953 and rallied a steel-bodied roadster (RUB 120), which was subsequently converted to a drop-head with two occasional rear seats to qualify it for a certain rally. Later, it was sold and was driven by Scott and Cunningham in the 1954 Alpine, as seen here.

172 mph! That was the speed recorded by the modified Special Equipment XK 120 roadster at Jabbeke in 1953. Note the blanking for the radiator and the brake-cooling slots, also bubble canopy for the driver, Norman Dewis, seen standing next to Lofty England on the left. Malcolm Sayer (in jacket) was responsible for the body modifications, and for the shape of the C/D prototype alongside, which achieved 178 mph that day.

The ex-Dick Protheroe XK 120 at Silverstone in the hands of later owner Rhoddy Harvey-Bailey. This has been one of the fastest and most active of XKs in club racing.

be recorded. The first concerned the newly-introduced fixed-head XK 120, an example of which (actually the second right-hand-drive car completed) was taken to the bumpy Montlhéry circuit in France during August 1952 for an epic long-distance run. The idea — not publicized before the start — was to circulate the car for seven days and seven nights at an average speed of over 100 mph. After a false start, when a tyre burst at some 120 mph, this was comfortably achieved, the closed XK averaging 110.31 mph for 16,851 miles, crewed by Leslie Johnson, Stirling Moss, Bert Hadley and Jack Fairman. This aroused much interest at the time, and several International long-distance records were broken during the run.

Then, in October 1953, a stripped and modified XK 120 roadster was taken to Jaguar's old hunting ground at Jabbeke, in Belgium, with results that startled even Jaguar. Test-driver Norman Dewis was at the wheel, and in conditions of dead calm, he took the XK down the autoroute to record an astonishing average speed of 172.412 mph. The car, carrying the registration number MDU 524 and thus apparently the XK 120 which Gatsonides and Samworth had driven in the 1952 Alpine Rally,

used a very high 2.92:1 final-drive, and the power was provided, it seems, by a very high-compression engine. The basic shape of the car was not altered at all, just the sidelights being removed and the brake-cooling slots and part of the radiator grille being blanked-off. 'We'd have been quite happy with 155 mph!', Mr England told me years later.

XK 120 competition successes extended spasmodically into the late-'fifties, by which time the car was too heavy and old fashioned to be a major force in anything except a few club formulae. Likewise, it was weight more than anything which prevented many notable results being recorded by its successors, the XK 140 and XK 150. The former, however, did have one chance of covering itself with a little bit of glory, on the occasion of the 1956 Le Mans race. Peter Bolton and Bob Walshaw entered their standard road-going XK 140 fixed-head coupe, with modifications being limited to a few days' preparation at Brown's Lane to fit a D-type head and a 36-gallon fuel tank. All the trim, including the walnut dashboard, was retained!

The coupe lapped discreetly, but deceptively quickly and it was soon well ahead of the equally standard Mercedes 300SL which

Another Protheroe-prepared XK 120, further modified by Robin Beck to the extent of shortening the wheelbase. The ex-rally car is being chased by one Jackie Stewart in Eric Brown's much-modified XK 120 drop-head, registered 1 ALL. Stewart won this particular battle at Crystal Palace in 1964.

The Bolton/Walshaw XK 140 at Le Mans, some time prior to its most regrettable disqualification, but for which it could well have finished in the first 10.

ran until its engine gave up, and by midday on the Sunday the Jaguar was in 11th place overall. Alas, there was a muddle over refuelling (the drivers had arranged little or no pits organization, and David Murray had to rescue them from complete chaos) and the French officials insisted on eliminating the car for taking on petrol after 33 laps instead of the regulation 34-lap period. Bolton and Walshaw were almost inconsolable, but there was nothing to do but pack up and go home. There are no 'ifs' in motor racing, but had the car continued it would probably have finished in ninth place overall, the highest of any XK at Le Mans.

This was not the only occasion on which a reasonably well-prepared XK 140 was shown to have the legs over Mercedes' complex and much-vaunted 300SL. 'Chuck' Wallace had beaten noted Mercedes driver Paul O'Shea in a superb drive at Hagerstown, USA, on his way to a 1955 SCCA C-Production class championship win for the second time (he had already won it in 1954 with an XK 120).

Racing results, however, were the exception rather than the rule, though the XK 140 did reasonably well in rallies. Ian Appleyard was now running a fixed-head XK 140 instead of RUB

120, the steel-bodied replacement XK 120 for his famous original car, which had gone into retirement after 1952 (RUB 120 ended-up with a two-plus-two drophead body, but was later broken-up). But his XK 140 made only the occasional appearance in rallies, and it was left to such as 'Bobby' Parkes to score consistently in this field with an XK 140.

It is even harder to find notable results when it comes to the XK 150. In 'S' form it may have had more power than its predecessors, but the factory had carried out no suspension development and the car simply could not match lighter and more modern opposition. Thus the GT class win (and 10th place overall) secured by Eric Haddon and his Austrian-born navigator Charles Vivian in the 1960 Tulip Rally stands out, their XK 150S roadster finishing ahead of one of the new 3.8 Mark 2 Jaguar saloons, at least one 300SL Mercedes, the Morley brothers' Big Healey and several Porsches. The XK 150 picked up maximum bonus points on the Mont Ventoux hill-climb, beating the Swann/Sager Aston Martin DB4 in the process. But Jaguar's rally mantle had really been picked up by the 3.4 saloons introduced back in 1957, and was to continue with great success

Eric Haddon and his Austrian co-driver Charles Vivian, having previously made a name for themselves in Haddon's XK 120 roadster RJH 400, were amongst the few to make a serious attempt at rallying the XK 150. Their best result was a 1960 Tulip Rally GT class win.

The XK 150 was quite often sprinted and hill-climbed by owners — sometimes a little too enthusiastically, it seems, judging from the antics of this fixed-head at Shelsley Walsh!

The most successful XK 120 in latter-day modified sports car racing was John N. Pearson's glass-fibre-bodied drop-head, a victor of many races. The car is seen here at a 1971 Silverstone meeting, between John Quick's well-known E-type and Mick Hill's 'Janglia' — a very rapid Jaguar —powered Ford Anglia 105E.

with the improved Mark 2 version during the first half of the 'sixties — to the exclusion even of the new E-type Jaguar which replaced the XK series, but which never had the factory backing necessary for it to build on its undoubted potential in this branch of the sport. In the United States, one of the few reasonable results for the XK 150 was gained early in its career when Walt Hansgen took a brand new XK 150S roadster (standard except for a roll-over bar) to third place behind a Cheetah (an MG special) and a Ferrari 250 coupe at the Bridgehampton circuit in 1958.

A few clubmen (and women!) persevered with the XK 150 on the track, where it could be made to go quickly, but was seldom a race winner. When, during the upsurge of interest in modified sports car racing during the late-'sixties and early-'seventies, it was the XK 120 to which people turned, John N. Pearson producing a frighteningly fast device which utilized a glass-fibre replica body on a much-modified XK 120 drop-head chassis. With a modified E-type engine, this car proved almost unbeatable in its division of club racing, E-types, Lotus Elans and Corvette Stingrays not withstanding, while in today's Thoroughbred sports car racing class for old production sports cars, the XK 120 in less altered form continues generally to reign supreme, its competition days far from over.

CHAPTER 6

Buying a Jaguar XK

The choice, the examination and the test

First of all, do you know what you're buying? If you've read the previous chapters you will know how the XK fared in its own time, but the last example left the factory over 20 years ago and things have changed a lot since then. Is the car impractical and unpleasant in today's conditions, supposing you can afford the prices being asked these days?

Well, anything is practical if you are hardy or eccentric enough — I know of people who still use prewar open tourers as their sole means of transport, and even the earliest XK 120 is more civilized than that. One point can be made clear from the start, however — thanks to a performance that was always so much ahead of its time, any XK will easily keep up with modern traffic, in or out of town, which is more than can be said of many cars of the 'fifties. Also, if not repeatedly caned, the brakes are adequate, too. So the main disadvantages the XK suffers in relation to a modern car lie in its ancilliary equipment, or lack of it — heating and demisting (if present) is feeble, the lights are nowhere near up to the performance, the steering is heavy in town and, in wet weather, the pathetic clap-hands wipers of the divided-windscreen cars can make life a misery.

Not that many XKs are bought or used now for everyday transport; most serve instead as weekend 'fun' cars with occasional longer trips to Jaguar Driver's Club rallies thrown in. A good number of each variety have now been rebuilt to concours standard, which gives us the pleasure of seeing them as they must have appeared on leaving the factory. Such examples are not, however, terribly usable, because energetic driving inevitably produces dust, dirt, oil marks and stone chips, undoing the work of countless evenings and weekends. True concours cars are

therefore best regarded as exhibits rather than exhilarating transport, and if you reckon to spend more time enjoying your XK on the road than polishing the underside, it is better to aim at acquiring a merely excellent car rather than a concours one.

Those generalizations apply to all three types of XK; as for whether to choose an XK 120, 140 or 150, this depends on your own taste and what you want to do with the car. The XK 120 obviously has the greatest historical appeal, and many prefer its cleaner lines. It handles virtually as well as its successors, and the 190-bhp car has a performance which can still be labelled 'fast'. A few parts are getting a little difficult to acquire, now, but this is not a determining factor and is unlikely to become one. The roadster version was the very first XK to become collectable, but the rarity of the fixed-head and drop-head cars has narrowed the gap now, and prices have evened-out.

The XK 140 was for a long time the poor relation of the XK family, having neither the historical attraction exerted by the XK 120, nor the more modern conveniences (like disc brakes) offered by the XK 150. Yet it is an exceedingly pleasant and practical car to drive, even in the most ordinary (if one can use that phrase about XKs these days) fixed-head coupe guise. The steering is precise, the car can be drifted round bends with great controllability, there is adequate room inside (even for a small family unless you choose the roadster), and, if you select an example with overdrive, cruising speed is whatever you like up to the maximum. Poor examples are still cheaper than equivalent-condition XK 120s, but when it comes to genuinely good cars, the price gap which used to exist between the types has closed, and a top-condition XK 120, 140 or 150 now fetches about the same money. Even the body style (open cars used to be much more expensive) affects values much less than it did.

If you want to use an XK with any degree of regularity, the XK 150, with its disc brakes and more modern fittings, is your best choice — some like the styling for its own sake, of course. Those disc brakes really are a huge advantage, particularly if you like driving XKs as they were meant to be driven. The latest of the XK line also offers a great deal of room, making it ideal for long-distance touring — some prefer it to the slightly cramped Series 1 and 2 E-types for that very reason. Or, if you are entering XK motoring on a tight budget, a rough XK 150 fixed-head — as the most common variety of XK to be found in this country — still represents the cheapest way to join the game.

There are many pitfalls, however, in buying an XK, whether you start at the top or bottom rung of the 'condition' ladder. High sums can be paid for a concours car that may not be so under the skin, while the purchaser of a semi-derelict car may well find that the size and complexity of restoration is way beyond his abilities and pocket. So a first essential is to get to know how to tell a good car from a poor one — assessing its value can come later, and depends largely on the state of the market at the time of purchase.

Rebuilding an XK from scratch is, as hinted above, difficult and expensive and should not be attempted by anyone who has not had considerable experience in tackling full rebuilds on 'lesser' cars. The mechanics are not the problem — it is the bodywork which sorts the men out from the boys. Even if you are a competent panel-basher and welder, it is unlikely that you will be able to get away without spending many hundreds of pounds on new or secondhand parts, particularly reproduction body panels and chrome trim items, which will almost certainly be necessary if the car is bought as a wreck. The subject of spares is discussed in the next chapter — if you have any doubts about what even a do-it-yourself restoration may cost, just contact one of the specialist suppliers and ask for a price list. A *professional* restoration is definitely only for the well-off — properly done, it will inevitably cost over £10,000 if the interior and mechanical parts of the car are to be renewed as well.

In fact, a professional restoration can rarely be justified on economic grounds, because the finished car is unlikely to be worth on the open market what you have spent on having the work done; the only consolation you will have is that (provided you manage to find a competent and conscientious workshop) you will *know* that the car is as good as it looks, with no hidden body damage, rust or filler. On a long-term basis things are not so bad — keep the restored car for three or four years and appreciation will take care of the matter.

So you will obtain better value for money by purchasing an already rebuilt (or perhaps better still, a mint low-mileage original) XK; but as this type of car is inevitably expensive, you must ensure that you get what you pay for — and there are still people who can and will achieve magnificent results with plastic filler covered by a top-quality spray job which will disintegrate into rust holes after a year or so. However, having decided to look at the car, it is a good idea (if the car looks promising at first glance) to begin by checking on points of originality, like ensuring it has the correct engine, cylinder-head, lights, bumpers and other fittings — so first examine closely the pictures and Appendices in this book!

By this time you will almost automatically have summed-up the XK's general appearance — do the body panels fit well, are there any ripples in the doors or those big front wings, and does the car stand correctly, without drooping to one side or at the rear? A lot of dirt and filth underneath and in the engine compartment almost certainly means neglect, and equally certainly will be covering up corrosion. Quite frankly, an expert can decide in a few minutes whether the car is genuine or not, just by mentally noting these few major points.

But a lot of money may be at stake, and you now need to close in and examine the car in detail. All steel-bodied XKs rust in approximately the same places, so regard the following procedure as reasonably standard. Start at the front and look for rust bubbles (or evidence of filler) under the headlight nacelles and around the sidelight housings (where these are integral with the wing). Look under the sidelight lenses, too, because the filler artist is sometimes careless about finishing off his handywork at this point, and may give himself away. Then feel along the bottom of the front wings and around the footwell ventilators where fitted. Also look for rot in the battery boxes contained in the front wings of XK 140s and 150s.

Then move on to the all-important door hinge pillars — you will not be able to see much of the actual hinges, but opening the door about nine inches and lifting it will betray any bad wear or

A home rebuild in progress — but not everyone has the skills and facilities necessary to undertake a worthy restoration. (Bob Kerr)

'drop'. Also, examine the outer wing where it hides the bulkhead ends for signs of bodged repairs — sometimes the front wing is cut away here to effect repairs to the hinges, and if it has not been properly welded back, the patch will soon rust and lift. Examine the bottoms of the pillar itself for rot, under where the bottom hinge disappears into it.

The sills which are disclosed on opening the door can be looked at next — anything on their outer faces will be visible at once, but also lie down and slide under the car to examine the inner faces — or at least feel for loose metal and holes with your hand. The rear door shut pillar, just in front of the rear wheels, is also notorious for rot on XKs, and often the closing panel in front of the rear wheel disintegrates completely. Beware of neat-looking aluminium plates here, which may cover all sorts of horrors.

Before leaving this area, see that the door catches and locks work properly — new parts are difficult to find.

Where the rear wings bolt on to the tonneau panel on XKs there should be a beading — and in body-colour, too, if you want to be particular. Examine either side of this beading for rust bubbles all the way round and look at the bottoms of the rear wings. On drop-head models (not roadsters) look very carefully at where the top meets the body, and lift up the material here to see if rot exists. The hood material is pinned to a wood frame, which runs all the way round the rear of the cockpit and readily attracts water, with subsequent rot — and in an expensive place, too. On fixed-heads, particularly XK 150s, look below the rear side windows — believe it or not, this area can rot for as much as 2 inches upwards from the rear wing/body join.

This is an XK drop-head under restoration, showing the metal above the rear wings which often suffers; on these models it is backed by wood, which attracts damp.

Vital points to check on an XK's body include the pillars either side of the door and the big sills. On XK 150s, rubber bungs can be removed for a look inside the latter.

Next, open the bootlid, lift the spare wheel compartment lid, remove the spare wheel and examine the well in which it sits. This rusts along its seams and where hollow stiffening pieces were spot-welded vertically on its sides — watch out for repair patches pop-rivetted over these areas. Is there a smell of petrol? A new tank costs well over £100 and the old one may be beyond repair. The bootlid on XK 150s rusts, so examine it along the bottom edges, and cars with steel doors suffer from rust — often they will have been inexpertly plated, the new steel reaching half-way up the outside of the door; this is unsatisfactory as the metal either flexes or rusts, with an unsightly line appearing on the door heralding big trouble. The lack of drain holes underneath the door is a good way to spot plating (though if the repair is taken up to beyond the curve of the door, it can be perfectly sound).

An XK 150 with a rear wing removed, showing the vulnerable door-closing pillar and large amounts of filler under the side window.

The spare-wheel well of an XK 150 under restoration. Be sure to check the floor and sides for rust or poor repairs.

The XK's chassis-frame is not prone to rust, but as all the variants are over 20 years old, the time has come when it is worth checking. The tendency is for rot, when it does occur, to manifest itself on the top, horizontal surface of the chassis-frame, where mud or water can lie. This is particularly true when it comes to the weakest part of the frame, that which curves over the rear axle and continues alongside the boot. This must be checked thoroughly. Sometimes, a radiator that has been leaking over a long period will cause the frame to rot through around the front suspension mounting points, but this is very rare.

While the bodywork of an XK is of overriding importance, do not dismiss a tatty interior, because to retrim it is expensive — this holds particularly true of the leather seats. Don't be fooled by new carpets (the cheapest cosmetic improvement of all to make, and neither here nor there when it comes to making a decision about a car), and if any retrimming has been carried out, is it to original specification? This is most important, as however good it may look, a non-original interior (or anything else come to that) will devalue the car considerably. The state of the top on a drop-

The most rust-prone area of the XK's chassis is the top surface of the part which sweeps over the rear axle. This example has gone just in front of the rear body mount.

head coupe is crucial, too, because to have a new one tailored and installed will cost hundreds of pounds — and the exterior fabric *must* be cloth, as opposed to the vynide which is permissible on roadsters (if only because it is cheaper to replace in the future).

Moving on to the mechanical aspects of an XK, at least one can say that one is dealing with known quantities (unlike bodywork repairs, which can range from a few pounds to thousands, depending on what is under the paintwork). So, if a car's engine is obviously 'duff', then you can allow for this in the purchase price to be negotiated.

Driving the car will tell you most about its mechanical condition. However, before you start up, take a look round the engine for signs of new gaskets and extra clean parts which may indicate recent work (or which, if absent, may refute the vendor's claim of such). Then get in the driving seat and check that all the needles are at 'O' — especially on the oil gauge. Start up and let the engine idle — did the oil-pressure gauge needle respond quickly and show a reasonable pressure on tickover, and is the

dynamo charging? Rev-up and look round for blue smoke from the exhaust. Listen for any strange noises in the engine before you move off, particularly bottom timing chain noise, which to repair is really an engine-out job. Some noise from the cylinder-head is to be expected — in fact an over-quiet head means the tappet clearances have closed-up too much, indicating improper or lack of maintenance.

As you engage the clutch, keep an ear open for any clunks from the rear-end, which on a wire-wheel car may indicate worn splines (expensive); a regular squeak when on the move could mean the same thing, or it could be loose spokes. Go up through the gears gently, taking particular note of any grating noises or excess whine from first (later, try reverse, too — both these gears are expensive to replace). Allow the engine to fully warm-up — it will take some miles — and ensure that at least 40 psi oil pressure is shown at between 2,500 and 3,000 rpm.

Don't expect there to be very much synchromesh action as you change gear, and there's a long travel, too, with this gearbox, but

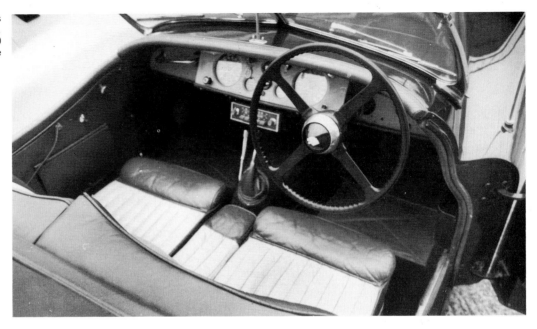

Interior condition is important, and so is originality if the car has been retrimmed. This is a very well preserved XK 120 roadster with the original upholstery; the only jarring note is the modern radio.

it should be virtually silent in third and top. Try a change from second to top at around 25-30 mph, then put your foot down — this should show-up any clutch slip. In general, the performance of the car should be sweet and willing right up to the red line on the rev counter — misfiring when fully warm indicates that something is wrong, probably a trivial thing like plugs or points, but possibly something worse like a stuck valve. Obviously there should be no bearing noise, though piston slap is not uncommon or particularly worrying if the engine has covered a considerable mileage. When it comes to judging mileage, unless it is a one-owner car, with complete documentation, don't listen to anything you're told on this subject, but make up your mind purely on the condition of the car — its general appearance, wear in the interior and so on (it's a good idea to ask yourself whether, if you had owned this car from new and covered this mileage, you would expect it to look like it is).

The steering, on both rack-and-pinion and recirculating-ball cars, should have only the smallest amount of lost movement at the wheel, or none at all — I would regard half-an-inch as excessive. Neither steering is light at low speeds, and the Burman steering can be heavy at high speeds, too. Beware of any clonks from the front suspension, and listen for rattles generally — like all cars with a separate chassis, the XK is not rattle-free, but you should be able to detect anything particularly noisy and find out why.

If you have not driven an XK before, you are, of course, at a disadvantage — it is difficult to make an accurate judgment about the car's behaviour if everything is strange to you, and for anyone used to modern cars, an XK takes some getting used to. For a start, it's big (almost as long as a Ford Granada) and the bonnet seems an inordinate length especially as the seating position is very low, with your legs stuck out in front of you parallel to the floor. The steering wheel seems massive, too, and you begin to wonder how on earth you can drive these things fast; Healey 3000 owners suddenly realize that 'big' should not be applied to their cars at all! The clutch travel is long, the gearchange slow (if you

Check carefully the condition of the steering, brakes and suspension, looking out for excessive play or stiffness on turning the steering wheel, brakes which pull or have worn discs, and wear in the suspension ball-joints, shown by excessive drop as the car's weight is taken off the assembly.

want it to be silent), and the brake pedal pressure (on the drum-braked cars) heavy, though the brakes should be perfectly capable of pulling the car up squarely and quickly.

But don't worry — get used to it all, and you will soon start to enjoy the attributes of the car, the smooth response of that magnificent engine, the beautiful change from top to third and back again (virtually the only gears you need once on the move), the roadholding, which will be far better than you initially realized, and the still remarkable degree of ride comfort for a sports car. Soon, operating the controls will become second-nature, and you will be enjoying that blend of smooth unstressed power, predictable handling and effortless progress which is unique to the XK. If you don't, then either the car is wrong, or you are just not cut out for XK motoring.

Assuming you have completed your test run, stop the engine and take another look under the bonnet — are there any new oil leaks (there's usually a bit of weeping from the cam covers), are there a lot of fumes coming from the breather pipe, and is any water being pushed out of the radiator? Contrary to popular opinion, XKs only overheat if something is wrong with the cooling system or engine. Allow the engine to cool and take a look at the radiator water — are there any signs of oil mixed in, which could mean a faulty head gasket? Check the dipstick, too, for emulsified oil, and undo the oil filler cap on the cam covers (with care — it will still be hot) and look inside for the same reason.

Finally, the condition of the front suspension should be checked; if possible, jack-up the car from under the bottom suspension member and note the amount of 'drop' given by the ball-joint. Watch for 'dry' grease nipples, which may indicate lack of maintenance. The inner suspension mountings are Metalastik joints, which do wear out — check for signs of the rubber separating from the metal and wearing oval. While in the area, check the condition of the rubber-bonded steering rack mountings on XK 140s and 150s.

So much for condition — what about prices? For obvious reasons actual amounts cannot be quoted here because they could change, but generally speaking it is condition which dictates what a car will fetch. All XKs, even total wrecks, have appreciated in value from their all-time low around 1967-8, when you could buy the very best for about £500, and as already mentioned earlier in this chapter, one phenomenon of the XK's rise in price has been

This picture shows a very badly worn top ball-joint on an XK suspension detached from the car. The dirt shield has virtually disintegrated and the ball has worn through its cup.

the levelling-out of values amongst the various types and body styles. Previously it was a safe bet to say that XK 120s were worth more than XK 150s, that XK 150s were worth more than XK 140s, and that the open versions of each fetched more money than the closed models. Now, condition and originality are better guides to ultimate value.

However, this does not mean that certain characteristics are not more desirable than others. If you could find a bunch of XKs in exactly the same concours condition, the ones with wire wheels, overdrive and — as appropriate — a C-type or straight-port head *should* be a more attractive proposition. Certainly they would be the most fun to drive — except that many owners these days rarely seem to drive briskly enough to appreciate these assets. Such extras do, however, exert a much stronger influence on the price of an XK lower down the condition scale, which still includes the majority of the cars.

If you are not all that familiar with XK Jaguars, get to know the cars by seeing as many as possible and chatting to their owners. An ideal way to do this is to join the Jaguar Driver's Club, which has an XK Register — even if you don't already own a Jaguar, becoming an Associate Member gives you most of the privileges, and you will be informed via the monthly *Jaguar Driver* magazine of the many rallies the club holds, where XKs are usually represented. The XK Register's major annual date, however, is International XK Day, where several hundred are to be seen. The club's address will be found in the Appendices.

When it comes to values, similar research is required and you will need to purchase copies of *Exchange & Mart, Motor Sport* and *Thoroughbred & Classic Cars* in particular to see how prices are going. *Practical Classics* magazine also publishes a unique price guide, which lists the values of XKs as well as many other classic cars. However, only by travelling to see the cars advertised will you be able to judge how their price matches their condition, and be prepared for disappointments as descriptions in private small-ads are notoriously unreliable. If long distances are involved, it is best to cross-question the vendor on the telephone first in an attempt to avoid a wasted journey, but even this precaution can sometimes prove misleading.

Buying from a dealer certainly need not be ruled out, and the more reputable ones specializing in this type of older Jaguar will usually describe the example for sale more accurately, will have checked it for roadworthiness at least, and may also offer after-sales service. Unless the car is exceptional, a firm guarantee is unlikely, simply because it is impossible to predict what may or may not happen with a car of this age. However, bear in mind it is the car you are buying, not the sales patter, and each example looked at must be judged on its own merits.

Happy hunting!

CHAPTER 7

Spares and maintenance

Sources, methods and modifications

Compared with a modern car, the XK Jaguar is a relatively simple machine with not a great deal to go wrong. For example, there is no independent rear suspension with lots of parts to wear out, or a complicated heating and ventilation system, or any emission-control equipment on the engine. The steel bodywork is by far the weakest part of the car, but even this is not structural.

The XK engine has a legendary reputation for longevity, and if anything the 3.4-litre and 3.8-litre versions which are to be found in XKs are tougher than the later 4.2-litre variants. Mileages of 100,000-200,000 are common between overhauls, with attention in the meantime being limited to oil changes, plugs and points. The engine's weakest point is probably its aluminium cylinder-head, which can suffer from corroded waterways, but this can usually be repaired by aluminium welding.

While you might not find them 'on the shelf', parts can be obtained for rebuilding even the earliest XK engines, which can often be updated with internals from later examples if desired. Or, if you are working to a budget, engines from virtually any of the Jaguar saloons can generally be fitted — although don't forget that this will devalue the car on originality grounds. Parts for a full XK engine rebuild can cost upwards of £500, while to have the work done by a specialist garage will take you into four figures.

If you are a competent home mechanic with a good basic toolkit, rebuilding an XK engine is probably within your capabilities, so don't be put off by the thought of six cylinders and twin overhead camshafts. It is a beautifully designed, logically built engine, and with a good manual to guide you, the work should be straightforward. It can be a good idea to order all the parts necessary from one Jaguar specialist, which should ensure you get the right items for your engine; you then also have a good source of advice when you come to put it all together! A couple of special tools are required, but these can usually be hired or borrowed.

The non-synchro Jaguar gearbox usually matches the engine for toughness, but when it does wear out, first and reverse gears generally go first; unfortunately, new gears are not available (at the time of writing) so even the specialist repairers have to adapt components from Mark 2 Jaguar saloon gearboxes as a last resort. Bearings and other parts are not difficult, however. The Laycock overdrive, where fitted, is inclined to be idiosyncratic, sometimes being slow to engage or disengage, with either the hydraulic or electric circuits being suspect. Spares and service can still be obtained, however.

The front suspension on all XKs is, to all intents and purposes, the same. It is very hard-wearing, with even the ball-joints lasting six-figure mileages, though only if regularly greased. The maintenance-free inner rubber mountings do succumb with age, but as with the ball-joints, new parts have been commissioned by specialist firms, so cost is the only important factor to be considered when rebuilding a worn torsion-bar suspension. Steering parts are also available, and often what appears to be a worn-out steering rack can be returned to service with only a change of bearings — so get specialist advice before plumping for an entire exchange unit.

On wire-wheeled XKs, the splined hubs can be a source of annoyance and expense; age, or more particularly lack of maintenance (it is essential to clean the splines regularly and re-

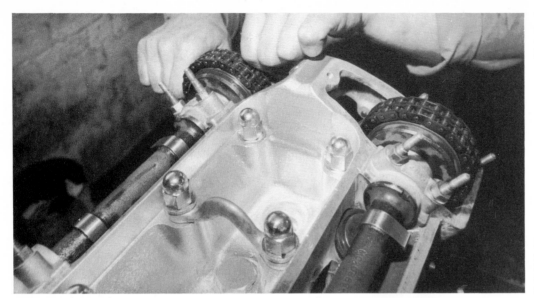

You need not be overawed by the XK engine, which is within the scope of the competent home mechanic to rebuild, given care and a little guidance.

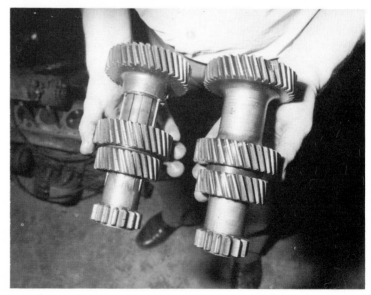

Few mechanical parts for XKs are totally unobtainable, and it seems certain that even expensive items like these gear clusters — now out of stock from the maker's — will be remanufactured.

apply clean grease) results in wear, which in turn can result in a wheel coming off or — conversely — refusing to shift from the hub! New splined hubs are available once more, but are expensive to buy and often a major job to fit — removing the old hubs can be a time-consuming and exhausting procedure.

Parts for an XK's braking system are generally available — that is, whereas you may not be able to locate (say) a new wheel or master cylinder for an early XK 120 *immediately,* you will probably be able to gather together what you need for a brake overhaul over a period of time. Spares for the disc-braked cars are much easier. As with any major job on an older car, the best policy is to stock up with parts before attempting the work, which will give you time to search out any difficult items.

When it comes to bodywork, take heed of what was said in the previous chapter — restoring an XK's metalwork is definitely *not* a beginner's job! If you do intend to have a go, you have one thing going for you, however, and that is the wide range of reproduction body parts which are now available. Some of these may have to be ordered in advance from a supplier (nothing for XKs, bar some engine and gearbox/suspension parts, are available

If you are set on rebuilding the bodywork of your XK at home, and the car is very poor, it will generally be found more satisfactory to buy a complete new rear-end, such as this unit marketed by Oldham & Crowther.

from BL any more), but you *can* arrive at a complete new bodyshell for an open XK 120, for instance. In fact, if you are restoring a very rusty car, much work and expertize can be avoided by purchasing a whole rear-end assembly, which should come complete with inner wings, tonneau panels and spare wheel well. This, plus new front and rear outer wings, is probably the easiest way to rebuild an XK body, and you will end up with a virtually new shell.

Many smaller repair panels are also available from specialist suppliers, as are door skins, sills, floors, bulkhead ends, sidelight pods and so on. Quality varies, so compare panels and prices before you commit yourself, and don't forget that even brand new factory panels (if you could get them) would require skilled fitting, so don't expect everything to slot together like a Meccano set.

One economical way of rebuilding an XK is to order panels in the way described, then prepare the car yourself and retain a welder to undertake the skilled work required. Or, you can strip out the car yourself, have the bodywork professionally restored, take it back as a repaired bare shell, and build-up the remainder of the car at home; this last job is as time-consuming (and thus as expensive) as the skilled metal work itself. In all cases, however, you should ensure that those who will be working on the car know what they are doing — always ask to see examples of their previous work, and speak to owners of cars they have restored. Take all estimates with a pinch of salt — very rarely does the final cost of the job not exceed the original amount quoted by a considerable degree.

Once the body has been repaired, the interior can be tackled; some of the original colours and textures of plastics for door trims, for example, are no longer available, but acceptable equivalents are usually to be found. Leather for the seats, of course, is no problem (except in finding the money) and the hides will come dyed to original specification. Trimming is something which can be learnt, but most people use a professional — choose one who knows XKs, otherwise you might end-up with an

The best way of dealing with badly rusted front wings is to replace them, but if you cannot afford that, repair sections, like this example for an XK 150 wing, are available.

unnecessarily unoriginal interior.

There is good news on the subject of exterior chrome-plated trim parts — almost everything for an XK 120, and an increasing amount for XK 150s (plus some XK 140 items), is now being reproduced — bumpers, grilles, rearlight units, bonnet badges and boot handles are typical items. Many of these come from the United States, where most XK restorations take place because more cars went there than remained in Britain. Rubber items, too, have become available once more, such as XK 120/140 roadster windscreen pillar grommets and various types of rubber extrusions for draught-sealing etc. Naturally such items (especially the plated ones) are not cheap, mainly because the quantities produced are comparatively small, but at least they are available to put the finishing touches to a good rebuild.

To sum up, the XK owner is generally well-off when it comes to spare parts, whether it be for simply maintaining a running car, or restoring a wreck. There are exceptions — and the situation changes almost monthly as 'old new' stock is uncovered, or new items commissioned — but on the whole the position is much healthier than it is for most high-performance cars from the 'fifties.

Lastly, a few words should be said about modifying XKs. As with most cars of their age and status, it is now unfashionable to depart from the standard factory specification, but there are always enthusiasts who want to improve on the original article in some way. They can be divided into two groups — one just wants to make the car more pleasurable for road use, the other wants to go racing.

Most countries now have special 'historic' race meetings, which usually contain races for which XKs are eligible, though generally speaking the modifications are restricted to approximately what was done to the car by racing owners in the 'fifties. This usually means the use of a C-type head, high-compression pistons, the 3/8-lift cam of course, and twin 2-inch SU carburettors. These, combined with careful assembly, a close-ratio gearbox and maybe a lower final-drive ratio (3.77 or 4.09), produce a very tolerably fast XK which is also ideal for road use. Aeroscreens help on faster circuits in particular, and some people just fit them for their attractive appearance.

Other categories of racing allow considerably greater modification. Thoroughbred sports car racing in the UK, and certain divisions of SCCA production sports car racing in the United States, give the owner the scope to build an engine which may develop close to 300 bhp, through the use of a big-valve, gas-flowed straight-port head, special manifolding and possibly three twin-choke carburettors, special pistons and many other smaller 'tweaks'. Wider wheels (limited to 6-inch rim width in Britain)

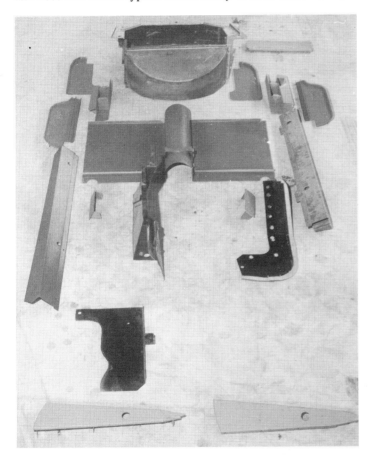

More replica body parts for XKs, including front bumper valances, sills, closing panels, floors, door pillars and complete spare-wheel well. *(Oldham & Crowther)*

When it comes to retrimming, care must be taken to use original-type materials and work to the proper patterns; this is original Jaguar trim on the door of a late XK 120 roadster. There are a number of firms who specialize in Jaguar trim if you are unable to do the job yourself.

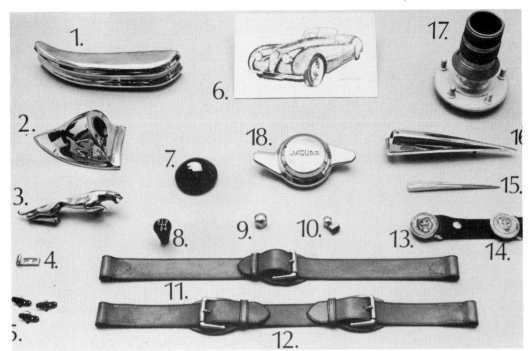

are normally allowed, and XKs in this state of tune are capable of 0-100 mph in 12 or 13 seconds. Bodywork exterior is required to remain almost standard, though.

This last restriction does not apply to Britain's Modsports (modified sports car) formula, which allows bigger wheelarches and extremely wide wheels, usually shod with 'slick' racing tyres. There have been a couple of very successful Modsports XKs, as mentioned in the competition chapter. An XK then becomes unsuitable for road use, however!

Needless to say, brakes and to an extent suspensions require updating, too, if the power output is to be increased. Disregarding true racing XKs, for road use a very effective conversion for XK 120s and XK 140s is to fit XK 150 discs all round. If you want to retain pressed-steel wheels, the disc brake units from the Jaguar Mark IX fit equally well (it is easiest to transfer the whole upright, including the hub).

When modifying a road-going XK there is, of course, the question of originality to be considered — it really depends on the use to which you want to put the car. If you enjoy using the performance to the full, disc brakes make the earlier cars much more fun to drive, but if you don't intend to tear about the countryside, the normal drum brakes are perfectly adequate and there is little point in changing them. Or, if you want to effect a compromise, fit them with Ferodo VG 95 linings, which are about the most fade-resistant available. In any case, changes to an XK's engine, suspension and brakes are generally of a bolt-on, bolt-off nature and so the car can easily be returned to standard at any time (provided the original parts have been kept). Alterations to the bodywork, however (flared wheelarches or extra louvres, for instance) are now almost universally frowned upon away from the race track.

Thanks to a sound original design, the XK's suspension copes remarkably well with large increases in horsepower, though some form of rear-axle location ('A' bar, or anti-tramp arms) is desirable if the level of tune exceeds normal C-type specifications. But just the substitution of telescopic dampers for the lever-type on XK 120s improves the behaviour of the rear-end considerably. Koni dampers are favoured in these circumstances, used in conjunction with a pair of the same make at the front. An extra leaf in the rear spring is sometimes used, together with a stronger (or additional) anti-roll bar on the front to counteract the oversteering tendencies this may produce. But all this is rather gilding the lily — XKs are fast and fun without any modifications at all!

The following people usually hold stocks of XK parts, though some specialize in only certain types of items:

Trevor Scott-Worthington, 'Gillingwood', Waste Lane, Berkswell, Warwicks. (Large range of reproduction/NOS chrome and accessory parts.)

Oldham & Crowther (Spares) Ltd, 27-31 Ivatt Way, Westwood Industrial Estate, Peterborough. Tel: Peterborough (0733) 262577/265021, Telex 32398. (Manufacturers and suppliers of body panels, repair sections, mechanical and trim parts. Worldwide service.)

Classic Autos, High Street, Kings Langley, Bucks. (Reproduction chrome parts and accessories; manufacturer of wings, etc.)

Suffolk & Turley, Unit 7, Attleborough Fields Industrial Estate, Garratt St, Nuneaton, Warwicks. Tel: Nuneaton (0682) 381429. (Retrimming to original standards.)

Vintage & Classic Spares Company, Lambert Works, Colliery Road, Wolverhampton, WV1 2RD. Tel: 0902 55561. (Lucas spares, including lights, spotlamps, ignition equipment, etc.)

Motor Wheel Services, 71 Jeddo Road, Shepherds Bush, London W12. Tel: 01-749 1391/743 3532. (New and rebuilt wire wheels.)

Bill Lawrence, 9 Badgers Walk, Dibden Purlieu, Hythe, Hants. Tel: Rownhams (0703) 733131. (Manufacturer of body panels, etc. Spares Secretary, XK Register.)

F.B. Components, 35-41 Edgeway Road, Marston, Oxford. Tel: Oxford (0865) 724646, Telex 83767. (Brake and suspension components a speciality. Worldwide service.)

Forward Engineering Co Ltd, Barston Lane, Barston, Solihull, West Midlands. Tel: Hampton in Arden (06755) 2163. (Engine reconditioning and engine overhaul kits; performance modifications.)

Woolies, off Blenheim Way, Northfields Industrial Estate, Market Deeping, nr Peterborough. Tel: Market Deeping (0778) 347347. (Trim materials.)

Ce Be Ee Components, Unit 11, Holly Park Mills, Calverley, Pudsey, West Yorkshire. Tel: 0532 573700. (Brakes, suspension, steering, some chrome parts.)

Phillips Garage, New Canal St, Digbeth, Birmingham B5 5RA. Tel: 021-643 0912. (Engine rebuilds and spares.)

The Clubs

In Great Britain, a section of the Jaguar Driver's Club exists for XK Jaguars — this is the XK Register, which the author co-founded in 1967/68 and which now has approaching 2000 members, including a number overseas. The Register organizes an annual 'XK Day' which sees cars arriving from all over Europe and publishes a monthly 'XK Bulletin' within the JDC's *Jaguar Driver* magazine. There is a spares secretary to assist members, and a number of advertisements for parts and services for the XK appear in the magazine each month. Membership of the XK Register is free on joining the JDC, and the address to write to for an application form is: Jaguar Driver's Club Ltd, 'Jaguar House', 18 Stuart St, Luton, Bedfordshire.

XK owners in North America can join one of the 45-odd Jaguar Clubs of North America affiliated local organizations, and up-to-date addresses of these can be obtained from JCNAS, 600 Willow Tree Road, Leonia, New Jersey 07605, USA. Australia contains some of the most enthusiastic XK owners, and up-to-date addresses of the Australian Jaguar clubs can be obtained from the British JDC, along with those of other Jaguar clubs the world over.

Technical specifications

XK 120

Engine: 6-cyl, 83 × 106mm, 3,442cc, CR 8:1 (7:1 & 9:1 optional), 2 1¾ in SU carbs, 160bhp at 5,000rpm (180bhp Special Equipment), maximum torque 195lb ft at 2,500rpm (203lb ft at 4,000rpm Special Equipment).
Transmission: Axle ratio 3.64:1 (ENV), later 3.54 (Salisbury — alternatives fitted include 4.09, 3.77, 3.27). Gearbox ratios: 12.29, 7.22, 4.98 (early), 11.95, 7.01, 4.84 (late).
Suspension and brakes: IFS by torsion bars and wishbones, anti-roll bar, telescopic dampers; live rear axle with leaf springs and lever-arm dampers. Burman recirculating-ball steering. Lockheed hydraulic two-leading-shoe front brakes with 12in drums front and rear. 6.00-16 tyres on 5in rims (5½ in later, pressed wheels only).
Dimensions: Wheelbase 8ft 6in; front track 4ft 3in; rear track 4ft 2in; length 14ft 6in; width 5ft 1½ in; height (OTS) 4ft 4½ in, (FHC) 4ft 5½ in, (DHC) 5ft 1½ in.
Basic UK price: £998 (OTS), £1,088 (FHC), £1,160 (DHC).

XK 140

As for XK 120 except:
Engine: 190bhp at 5,500rpm, 210lb ft at 2,500rpm (standard), 210bhp at 5,750rpm, 213lb ft at 4,000rpm (C-type head). Axle and gearbox ratios as for late XK 120 plus overdrive (where fitted) giving 3.19:1.
Rear suspension: telescopic dampers.
Steering: rack-and-pinion.
Dimensions: Length 14ft 8in; width 5ft 4½ in; height 4ft 7in (FHC).
Basic UK price: £1,127 (OTS); £1,140 (FHC); £1,160 (DHC).

XK 150

As for XK 140 except:
Engine: 190bhp at 5,500rpm, 210lb ft at 2,500rpm (standard); 210bhp at 5,500rpm, 216lb ft at 3,000rpm (Special Equipment); 3 2in SU carbs, 250bhp at 5,500rpm, 240lb ft at 4,500rpm ('S' model). 3,781cc, 87 × 106mm engine: 220bhp at 5,500rpm, 240lb ft at 3,000rpm (standard); 3 2in SU carbs, 265bhp at 5,500rpm, 260lb ft at 4,000rpm ('S' model).
Brakes: Dunlop disc with servo assistance, 12in diameter front and rear.
Dimensions: Length 14ft 9in; width 5ft 4½ in; height 4ft 6in (OTS).
Basic UK price: £1,175 (3.4 FHC); £1,457 (3.4 FHC); £1,195 (3.4 DHC); £1,477 (3.4S DHC); £1,457 (3.8 FHC); £1,535 (3.8S FHC); £1,390 (3.8 DHC); £1,555 (3.8S DHC); £1,175 (3.4 OTS); £1,457 (3.4S OTS); £1,457 (3.8 OTS); £1,535 (3.8S OTS).

Chassis Numbers, Engine Numbers and model identification

Chassis Number sequences

Model	Type	Period built	First Chassis No.	
			Rhd	Lhd
XK 120	OTS	July 49-Sept 54	660001	670001
	FHC	Mar 51-Sept 54	669001	679001
	DHC	Apr 53-Sept 54	667001	677001
XK 140	OTS	Oct 54-Feb 57	800001	810001
	FHC	Oct 54-Feb 57	804001	814001
	DHC	Oct 54-Feb 57	807001	817001
XK 150	OTS	Mar 58-Oct 60	820001	830001
	FHC	May 57-Oct 61	824001	834001
	DHC	May 57-Oct 60	827001	837001

Engine Number sequences

XK 120: From W.1001 to W.9999, then from F.1001

XK 140: From G.1001
XK 150: From V.1001 (standard 3.4)
From VA.1001 (standard 3.8)
From VS.1001 (3.4S)
From VAS.1001 (3.8S)
On all models Engine Number suffix /7, /8 or /9 indicates CR.

Specification identification

'S' prefix to XK 120 Chassis No. denotes Special Equipment model.
'A' prefix to XK 140 Chassis No. denotes Special Equipment model with standard cylinder-head.
'S' prefix to XK 140 Chassis No. denotes Special Equipment model with C-type head (also denoted by suffix 'S' on Engine No.).
'DN' suffix on XK 140 and XK 150 Chassis No. denotes that overdrive is fitted.

'BW' suffix on XK 140 and XK 150 Chassis No. denotes that automatic transmission is fitted.

'E' after the prefix 'JL' on XK 140 gearbox indicates that overdrive is fitted, as does 'S' after prefix on XK 150 gearbox; 'CR' suffix on 'JL' gearbox indicates close-ratio gears.

Location of numbers

Chassis, body, engine and gearbox numbers are found collectively on a plate fixed to the bulkhead in the engine bay. If the plate is genuine and the car retains its original components the numbers should correspond with those stamped on the individual components as follows:

Chassis: Stamped on top of chassis-frame opposite flywheel housing and sometimes on front cross-member under radiator.

Engine: Stamped on left-hand side of block above oil filter asembly and at front of cylinder-head casting.

Gearbox: Stamped on boss at left-hand rear of unit.

Body: Stamped on plate attached to left-hand side of bulkhead in engine bay.

APPENDIX C

Engineering changes — by model, date and number

The following data lists the changes in specification made to the XK series during the years of production, and will be of particular help to those restoring an XK to original 'factory' condition.

XK 120

Engine, gearbox and ignition

Aug 49	Engine oil level raised due to cavitation on rapid acceleration when oil cold; total capacity now 29 pints — low level on dipstick equates to old high level.
	Timing gauge introduced to toolkit. Part No. C.3993, or C.4015 in case-hardened steel for dealers' workshop use.
Dec 50	Individual air cleaners standardized. Part Nos. C.4496 and C.4732.
Nov 51	Mk VII-type stepped sump fitted, 24 pints total, Engine No. W.3593-96 and from W.3635.
Feb 52	Revised timing chain tensioner fitted from W.4052.
	Short mainshaft gearbox (SL or JL) without rear extension fitted, plus longer propeller shaft and speedo cable. Not interchangeable with Mk VII short-shafted box or long-shaft SH/JH boxes. With exceptions from:

OTS	FHC
660935 RHD	669003 RHD
671797 LHD	679215 LHD

Apr 52	Cylinder-head valve guides modified to fit 3/8in cam without further alterations, from W.4483.
	Mk VII-type oil-filter assembly, Part No. C.4767, fitted from W.4383.
May 52	Six-bladed high-speed fan and integral fan pulley and hub fitted from W.5465. Water-pump assembly interchangeable with Mk VII from A.2001, but not fan — XK 120-type smaller.
Oct 52	Oil-sump level indicator and element deleted from W.6149. Sump blanking plate and gasket fitted.

	Modified gearbox top cover (C.6878) and reverse striking rod from JL.13154. Only top interchangeable.
	Auxiliary starting carburettor switch — plunger modified.
Dec 52	Stop pin fitted to 1st and 2nd synchronizing sleeve to prevent over-travel on engagement of 1st gear with possible release of synchro balls and springs from JL.13834/SL.6313A.
Feb 53	W.O.2 needles replace R.F. in fixed-head coupe (weaker, giving better fuel consumption).
Mar 53	Modified water pump fitted from W.7207.
	Special Equipment fixed-head now fitted single exhaust system:
	669005 RHD 680738 LHD
May 53	Malleable-iron crankshaft damper replaces cast-iron from W.8381. Lightened flywheel (as for Special Equipment and C-type cars) fitted to all XK 120s from W.8275.
June 53	Modified con-rods with cap bolt bosses of increased length fitted from W.8643.
Aug 53	All cars now fitted with ignition suppressors.
Sept 53	Tappet settings revised on engines with 3/8in camshaft. Strengthened change-speed forks fitted from JL.18457/SL.9984A.
Nov 53	F.1001 Engine No. series commences.
Jan 54	Revised tappet settings for all cars, now 004 inlet/006 exhaust (006/010 competition use).
Apr 54	Modified inlet valve with depression in head fitted, interchangeable in sets from F.2365. Modified exhaust valves (no counterbore) and shortened guides fitted from F.2421.
May 54	Modified timing-chain tensioner, hard chrome-plated and polished, fitted from F.2773.

Suspension and rear axle

Jan 50	Threaded bearings either end of track-rod replaced by non-lubricated rubber bushes.

Aug 50	Castor angle now 3 degrees positive instead of 5 degrees positive:		
	OTS	FHC	
	660126 RHD	670439 LHD	

Nov 52	Salisbury axle, 3.77, fitted to certain cars:		
	OTS	FHC	
	660935 RHD	669003 RHD	
	671797 LHD	679222 LHD	

Dec 52	Stiffer rear springs, C.5721, as for SE models fitted standard:		
	OTS	FHC	
	661040 RHD	669003 RHD	
	673320 LHD	679222 LHD	

Apr 53	4HA 3.54 axle fitted instead 2HA 3.77 from:		
	OTS	FHC	DHC
	661054 RHD	669007 RHD	667002 RHD
	673695 LHD	680880 LHD	677016 LHD

Wheels and brakes

Dec 50　Blanking plates C.4292 now issued with each car in place of stoneguards C.3527 on air scoops to front brakes, for use when car is operated only at reasonable speeds in damp conditions.

Jan 51　Mintex M.14 brake linings replace M.15; higher pedal pressures resulting can be mitigated by drilling new holes for master cylinder yoke 2 5/8in from brake pedal fulcrum.

Apr 52	Self-adjusting front brakes and tandem master-cylinder fitted:		
	OTS	FHC	
	660980 RHD	669003 RHD	
	672049 LHD	679622 LHD	

May 52　5 ½ in wheel rims fitted (pressed wheels only).

June 53　Mintex M.20 linings fitted, including from drop-head coupe on commencement.

Sept 54	Modified handbrake lever fitted:		
	OTS	FHC	DHC
	661170 RHD	669185 RHD	667271 RHD
	675763 LHD	681471 LHD	678390 LHD

Body and equipment

Nov 51	Footwell ventilators fitted to front wing sides:
	660675 RHD
	671097 LHD

Nov 51	Air conditioning (without demist and defrost) now standard:
	660911 RHD　　671493 LHD

Oct 52　Demister vents now fitted at base of screen and connected to heater unit by flexible hoses (previously only fitted on fixed-head coupe):
660911 RHD　　672963 LHD
Sidelamp housings now incorporated in wings and cars for

export wired for flashing indicators (using existing lamp units):
661025 RHD　　672963 LHD

Dec 52　Synthetic enamel paint used from F.5272 (OTS) and J.2375 (FHC), also certain earlier batches.

Dec 52	Trico vacuum-operated windscreen washer fitted from (plus few cars previously):	
	OTS	FHC
	661037 RHD	669003 RHD
	673009 LHD	680271 LHD

Detachable plate fitted on right-hand side of gearbox cover to allow easy access to front UJ and spline nipples.

Jan 53　Zipping-type hood rear-view panel fitted:
661046 RHD　　673396 LHD

Apr 53　Continental Touring Kit available on sale or return, Part No. SD.1024, home market only.

June 53　Modified speedo cable fitted.

Sept 53　Racing screens and cowls previously supplied as standard with SE open-two-seaters now available to special order only.

Jan 54	Modified cigar lighter C.5631 ('Mk 2') with four indents on chrome-plated shoulder and element with copper-plated (previously silver) ejection ring fitted. Interchangeable as complete assembly only:		
	OTS	FHC	DHC
	661151 RHD	669106 RHD	667161 RHD
	674415 LHD	681271 LHD	678085 LHD

Aug 54　New reflector requirements, home market — two required, fitted either side numberplate, Part No. C.8746.

Sept 54	Rev. counter cable now completely black polythene outer sleeve:		
	OTS	FHC	DHC
	661165 RHD	669158 RHD	667243 RHD
	674929 LHD	681466 LHD	678305 LHD

	Flat horn-push (C.5558) fitted instead of dome-type (C.4514):		
	OTS	FHC	DHC
	661172 RHD	669194 RHD	667280 RHD
	675926 LHD	681481 LHD	678418 LHD

XK 140
Engine, gearbox and ignition

Feb 55　Rotor-type oil pump and circular oil seal at front of crank fitted, pressure relief valve fitted in filter head, from G.1908.

June 55　W.O.2 needles replace S.L. on C-type head cars from G.3250 and some cars prior.

	Relay incorporated in electrical circuit for operation of overdrive:		
	OTS	FHC	DHC
	800031 RHD	804121 RHD	807113 RHD
	811382 LHD	814216 LHD	817426 LHD

Sept 55	Hydraulic spring-loaded Reynolds lower tensioner replaced spring-bladed type; block revised to provide oil feed to chain via tensioner. From G.4431 on, plus 4411-4420.
Dec 55	Modified cylinder-head with reduced-depth tapped holes for new short studs on inlet face (short studs suitable for earlier heads) from G.6233.
	Modified oil filter (head of centre bolt at bottom of cannister instead of on top of filter head) from G.6233.
	Overdrive throttle switch fitted, preventing change from o/drive to direct top if car decelerating with closed throttle:

OTS	FHC	DHC
800062 RHD	804523 RHD	807319 RHD
811866 LHD	815252 LHD	818193 LHD

Apr 56	Tapered-periphery compression rings and modified oil-control rings fitted from G.7229.
	Modified exhaust valves and guides fitted, now common with C-type head, from G.6678.S.
Feb 57	Cylinder-head gasket now steel (C.7861) instead of Klingerite and Cupro nickel.

Suspension, rear axle and brakes

June 55	Modified rear-wheel cylinders fitted.
Sept 55	Castor angle changed from 2½-3 degrees positive to 1½-2 degrees positive to reduce kick-back.
Apr 56	Larger drive-gear bolts fitted to rear axle.
Jan 58	Servo-assistance kit introduced, Part No. 7076, for owners preferring less effort to operate brake pedal.

Body and equipment

| Sept 56 | Fly-off handbrake fitted: |

OTS	FHC	DHC
800072 RHD	804767 RHD	807441 RHD
812647 LHD	815755 LHD	818729 LHD

| Oct 56 | Doors on fixed-head and drop-head cars now steel instead of alloy: |

FHC	DHC
804781 RHD	807447 RHD
815773 LHD	818796 LHD

XK 150

Engine, gearbox and ignition

July 57	Hydraulic tensioner filter fitted from V.1191 (retrospectively if required).
Sept 57	Dynamo speed increased by smaller pulley (shorter fan belt required) from V.1599.
	Larger inlet valve guides fitted from V.1281 (interchangeable in sets).
Nov 57	Modified oil-pressure relief valve (with stop pin to limit travel of

valve and longer, lighter spring) fitted from V.2011.

	Five bottom setscrew hole bosses on timing cover machined to same length, previously one short and four long, from V.1921.
Nov 57	Synthetic rubber-bonded timing chain dampers replace nylon type (interchangeable). From V.2029.
	Automatic gearboxes manufactured in England from JBX 1001.
Apr 59	Lead-indium bearings introduced from V.6709. Mechanically engaged overdrive fitted, LHD roadsters only, from 831963 (later standard on 'S' models, optional on others).
May 59	Single air cleaner with paper element replaced three separate wire-mesh units on 'S' models:

OTS	FHC	DHC
820039 RHD	824864 RHD	827355 RHD
832076 LHD	836187 LHD	838246 LHD

June 59	Strengthened clutch slave cylinder bracket fitted from C.15709.
June 59	New cylinder-block for 3.4 (C.15950).
Nov 59	Exhaust pipes now clipped to silencers instead of welded.
Jan 60	Improved sump sealing — modified rear cover assembly with eccentric oil seal groove and new cork rubber seal at rear of cylinder-block: from V.7460; VA.1399; VS.2183; VAS.1085.
Mar 60	New piston 3.8, VA.1543 (note: 3.8S cylinder-head not chamfered at bottom of combustion chamber and requires piston crown of special design — C.14806/1 — to avoid fouling.
Apr 60	Tab washers instead of shakeproof type fitted to two setscrews which secure intermediate timing-chain damper.
	New-type 9:1 CR piston with domed instead of flat top fitted on 3.4 engine, from V.7524 and VS.2195.
Nov 60	Modified bearing material for 3.4, 3.8 and 3.8S.
	Modified cylinder-block, 3.8 engine, with repositioned boss to allow fitment of Bray engine heater from VA.2053 and VAS.1285.
Feb 61	Pressure die-cast timing cover and modified small-end bearings fitted from V.7656, VS.2212, VA.2202 and VAS.1293.
	Guide tube fitted to dipstick aperture from VA.2260.

Suspension, wheels and brakes

| Sept 57 | 1¾ in instead of 1 3/8in pistons fitted in rear brake calipers: |

FHC	DHC
824023 RHD	—
834454 LHD	837014 LHD

| Feb 58 | Cast-iron instead of aluminium master-cylinder body. |
| June 58 | 60-spoke wheels replace 54-spoke on all wire-wheeled cars (some cars fitted 60-spoke earlier). |

July 58	Nylon interleaving on rear springs introduced:		
	OTS	FHC	DHC
	—	824551 RHD	827168 RHD
	830960 LHD	835671 LHD	837573 LHD
May 59	Quick-change (square) brake pads introduced:		
	820004 RHD	824669 RHD	827236 RHD
	831712 LHD	835886 LHD	837836 LHD
June 59	Modified upper wishbone ball-joints with larger-diameter ball and increased angle of movement fitted:		
	OTS	FHC	DHC
	820004 RHD	824668 RHD	827234 RHD
	831968 LHD	835882 LHD	837831 LHD
July 59	Reservac fitted:		
	OTS	FHC	DHC
	820017 RHD	824742 RHD	827272 RHD
	831899 LHD	835935 LHD	837941 LHD
Aug 59	Brake fluid supply tank with level indicator and tell-tale light in cockpit fitted:		
	OTS	FHC	DHC
	820071 RHD	825179 RHD	827540 RHD
	832120 LHD	836744 LHD	838754 LHD

Body and equipment

Nov 57	Upper steering column modified to provide more positive locking of steering wheel. 50-amp fuses replace 35-amp in certain circuits.

May 58	Armrest on door modified to act as door pull:		
	FHC	DHC	
	824253 RHD	827011 RHD	
	835301 LHD	837332 LHD	
June 58	Direction indicator control transferred from dashboard to stalk on steering column:		
	FHC	DHC	
	824414 RHD	827069 RHD	
	835548 LHD	837415 LHD	
July 58	Rheostat switch fitted to allow control of heater motor, positioned adjacent to rev. counter and marked 'Heater, Fast-Slow':		
	OTS	FHC	DHC
	—	824420 RHD	827072 RHD
	830439 LHD	835566 LHD	837434 LHD
Apr 59	New rear bumper assembly fitted with overriders set further apart:		
	OTS	DHC	
	820001 RHD	827209 RHD	
	831250 LHD	837662 LHD	
June 59	Ashtray transferred from door casings to gearbox cover:		
	OTS	FHC	DHC
	820014 RHD	824702 RHD	827258 RHD
	831825 LHD	835905 LHD	837865 LHD
June 59	Electric rev. counter fitted:		
	OTS	FHC	DHC
	820043 RHD	824905 RHD	827373 RHD
	832088 LHD	836233 LHD	838272 LHD
Nov 60	Straight-cut pile carpet replaced curly-pile carpet on some cars.		

APPENDIX D

XK colour finishes

Few people find difficulty in identifying the correct Jaguar colour for painting the exterior of their XK, but when it comes to determining what colour or finish an individual component should have, there is often confusion. The following notes, although not definitive, may be of help.

ALL MODELS
Wheels
On all models, the pressed-steel wheels were body-colour. Wire wheels were also normally finished in body-colour, but chromium plating was an option — either the whole wheel or just spokes and hubs, the rim being varnished aluminium paint.

Hub-caps
Fitted to all pressed-steel wheels (including at the rear, where spats were always fitted on non-wire-wheeled cars). On XK 120s, the recessed areas of the hub-cap were painted body-colour, a practice discontinued by the time the XK 140 entered production. There were 'late' and 'early'-type hub-caps, but the difference is minimal. The 'Jaguar' nameplate should have a black background.

Wing beading
The piping between rear wings and body should be body-colour, as should the beading between front bumper valance and wings on XK 140s and XK 150s.

Numberplates

Export cars varied, but on all home-market XKs these fitted the rear backplates exactly and were never 'ribbed' at the edges. Most were of the 'Ace' variety; either pressed-aluminium or separate letters and figures were used.

XK 120

Bumper brackets

These varied, but generally speaking darker-coloured cars had the front and rear bumper brackets painted black, but others (*eg* white and silver) often had them painted body-colour. All the visible nuts attaching the bumpers and brackets were domed and chromium-plated, as were the spacers between body and bracket at the rear of the car.

Reversing light

The Lucas model 469 reversing/numberplate lamp was completely chromium-plated; the rear mounting bracket was normally painted body-colour.

Rearlights

The rearlight bodies were chromium-plated, except for a short period during 1951/52 when some cars left the factory with body-colour lamps due to a national shortage of nickel.

Front sidelights

The separate type were chromium-plated and seated on a flanged rubber 'gasket' (as were the rear lights).

Windscreen pillars

The entire windscreen assemblies on roadsters were chromium-plated, including the alloy pillars.

Interior and upholstery

Most early XK 120s had two-tone seats, the darker colour being the outside one to which the carpets and door trim were matched. The exception appeared to be cars finished in silver, when the seats and all interior trim were red, though later, suede green, pastel green and British racing green cars usually came with single-colour seats (suede green, or, in the case of BRG cars, that or tan). Where duo-tone upholstery was employed, the beading around the base of the dashboard matched the outer colour of the upholstery. Bear in mind that the factory would produce virtually any colour or trim combination to special order, however. All fixed-head and drop-head cars (except special-order ones) and many later roadsters had upholstery of one colour.

The seat frames of earlier XK 120s were chromium-plated, as were the hood-frame and sidescreen surrounds. All XK 120 roadsters had narrow rear windows with 'D' shaped ends — the plated rear window frame had four rubber grommets on the inside to prevent chafing of the hood material when folded. On later cars (see Production Changes) the window was contained in a zip-down panel; later cars had tops which anchored further back on the rear tonneau panel, nearer the bootlid. The shallow compartment under the rear tonneau panel, which held the sidescreens when not in use, was lined.

The right-angled part of the doors which covered the sills was normally covered by the same colour of vinyl as was used for the door trim panel.

Underbonnet

The usual underbonnet and bulkhead finish for all body styles appeared to be black, including in front of the radiator. However, some cars seem to have been finished in body-colour, or even left in red oxide primer. The inside of front and rear wings was normally 'blown over' with a thin coat of black paint, although the base colour of the whole bodyshell, inside and out, was body-colour. The underside of the bonnet was also body-colour (not black, or polished aluminium!). Bonnet and bootlid props were chromium-plated on earlier cars. The chassis-frame, rear axle, petrol tank, front suspension including dampers, track-rod arms and steering column were all black, as were brake drums on pressed-wheel cars. Boot (trunk) sides were painted black and so was the cover protecting the fuel-filler pipe and the spare wheel bay. Boot hinges were body-colour, as was the finisher panel running across the rear of the boot above the spare wheel bay.

As for individual underbonnet components, the cylinder-heads were painted as per the list included elsewhere. The alloy fan on early cars was not painted, but the later steel-bladed fans were painted black except for the outer 3 or 4 inches of the blades, which were silver. All alloy parts on the engine were unpainted; cylinder-block, crankshaft damper and pulleys and cast-iron gearbox casing were black. The dynamo body was silver, but the ends and bracket were black. The brake fluid reservoir was painted black, except for the cap, which was normally tin-plated. The air cleaners were painted black.

Exhaust system

On early roadsters, this ended on the left-hand side of the car, approximately mid-way between the rear of spat and end of the rear wing, and was cut off at an angle to match the contour of the wing. The system was given a coat of black paint (including the downpipes in the engine bay) except that the last few inches of the tailpipe had a bright finish, probably chromium-plated. Some time after the introduction of the fixed-head coupe (early fixed-heads had the 'slanted' tailpipe) the system was rerouted to end just inboard of the left-hand overrider, under the boot, but projecting to end about level with the overrider. It was straight-cut and the last few inches were plated. The twin-pipe system ended in approximately the same place, but was not plated.

XK 140

Broadly speaking, finish on the XK 140 followed XK 120 lines, though the following exceptions apply. Underbonnet finish was normally body-colour, though individual components were as for the XK 120, and the upholstery was always in one colour except to special order. Roadster hoods were as for late XK 120s, with the same size window in a zip-down panel, and roadster windscreens are also interchangeable with steel-bodied XK 120s. Standard XK 140s had the single exhaust pipe protruding between overrider and numberplate on the left-hand side of the car, and Special Equipment cars had the two exhaust pipes separated, one under each overrider. Both types of system had plated tailpipes. The luggage compartment sides were trimmed in Hardura (plastic-covered felt), the cover round the petrol pipe was carpeted, while the floor was covered by Hardura or carpet. The spare-wheel bay was body-colour except for the spare-wheel mounting bracket and the detachable, curved, forward part of the well, which were both painted black. The boot and bonnet stays were painted body-colour.

XK 150

Underbonnet and chassis finish applies as for the XK 140, and the exhaust system arrangements (single and twin) are also the same.

Cylinder-head — all models

The following chart shows the colours Jaguar painted the cylinder-head (in the plug wells and below the cam covers on each side), together with a brief specification of each different head. However, paint is easily changed, so check the cylinder-head number before relying on colours alone for identification!

Colour	Model employed on	Camshaft lift (in)	Exhaust valve diameter (in)	bhp
Silver	XK 120 standard and SE	5/16 (standard), 3/8 (SE)	1 7/16	160/180
Green	XK 140 standard	3/8	1 7/16	180
	XK 150 standard	3/8	1 7/16	190
Red	XK 140 C-type	3/8	1 5/8	210
Sky blue	XK 150 3.4 B-type	3/8	1 5/8	210
Metallic blue	XK 150 3.8 B-type	3/8	1 5/8	220
Gold	XK 150 'S' 3.4 straight-port	3/8	1 5/8	250
	XK 150 'S' 3.8 straight-port	3/8	1 5/8	265

Note: Inlet valves always remained at 1¾ in. Brake horsepower figures are gross and are provided for comparison purposes only; they also varied according to compression ratio (standard usually 8:1, optional 7:1 or 9:1).

APPENDIX E

XK production figures

Right-hand-drive/Left-hand-drive breakdown of XK production

Model	OTS	FHC	DHC
XK 120	1175/6437	194/2484	294/1471
XK 140	73/3281	843/1965	479/2310
XK 150	92/2173	1368/3094	662/2009

Note: XK 140 production totals include 396 fixed-heads and 385 drop-heads with automatic transmission. A breakdown of XK 150 production by engine and optional overdrive or automatic transmission is as follows:

		3.4	3.8	3.4S	3.8S
OTS	Auto	71	1	—	—
	O/drive	489	30	888	36
FHC	Auto	674	197	—	—
	O/drive	1651	334	199	150
DHC	Auto	440	209	—	—
	O/drive	789	264	104	89

Note: Discrepancies, not usually exceeding 10 units, may be found in totals derived from the above chart and from the RHD/LHD breakdown; the former figures have been taken from sales records, the latter from Chassis Number listings. The exact reasons for the variance are not always known, but may be due to certain cars being retained by the company, then not sold but broken up, chassis sent to specialist coachbuilders, or cars have re-allocated numbers. Final totals for the XK series, taken from sales records, are:

XK 120	12,078
XK 140	8,884
XK 150	7,929
XK 150S	1,466
	30,357

APPENDIX F

How fast? How economical? How heavy?

	XK 120 OTS	XK 120 FHC	XK 120 DHC	XK 140 OTS	XK 140 FHC	XK 150 FHC	XK 150 3.4S OTS	XK 150 3.4S FHC	XK 150 3.8S FHC
Mean max. speed (mph)	120	120	119	121	129	123	136	132	136
Acceleration (sec)									
0-30	4.0	3.3	3.5	2.7	3.2	2.8	2.5	2.9	3.4
0-40			5.3	4.2		4.5	4.0	4.5	
0-50	8.3	7.5	7.1	6.5	7.5	6.5	5.6	6.1	6.2
0-60	12.0	9.9	9.5	8.4	11.0	8.5	7.3	7.8	7.6
0-70	15.5	13.7	12.5	12.1	14.2	11.4	10.0	10.6	
0-80	19.0	17.1	16.9	15.7	16.9	15.0	13.0	13.2	12.8
0-90	25.9	22.1	23.3	19.6	22.7	19.5	16.4	16.5	
0-100	35.3	28.2	31.0	26.5	29.5	25.1	21.4	20.3	19.0
0-110			40.9		37.7	33.5		25.6	22.2
0-120								36.2	27.8
Standing ¼ mile		17.3	17.5	16.6	17.4	16.9	15.1	16.2	16.0
Axle ratio		3.77	3.54	3.54	4.09	4.09	4.09	4.09	4.09
Direct top accleration									
10-30	7.8	7.9			7.9	7.4		6.4	
20-40	7.5	7.7			7.5	6.4		6.4	
30-50	7.8	7.3			7.4	6.2		6.1	
40-60		7.4			7.7	6.3		6.3	
50-70		7.9			8.3	6.5		6.7	
60-80		8.1			9.4	7.1		6.3	
70-90		9.3				8.0		6.5	
80-100		10.9			11.5	10.2		7.4	
90-110						13.8		9.1	
Overall fuel consumption		17.5	16	18	21	20.5	17	18.6	13
Kerb weight (cwt)	26	27	27½	27	28	28¾	28½	28¾	28¾

The performance figures quoted on this page are reproduced through the courtesy of John Bolster *(Autosport)*, *Autocar*, *Motor* and *Road & Track* magazines.